ENGLISH UNIVERSITIES IN CRISIS

Markets without competition

Jefferson Frank, Norman G̶ ̶ar
and Michael Na̶

BRISTOL
UNIVERSITY
PRESS

First published in Great Britain in 2019 by

Bristol University Press
1-9 Old Park Hill
Bristol BS2 8BB
UK
t: +44 (0)117 954 5940
www.bristoluniversitypress.co.uk

North American office:
c/o The University of Chicago Press
1427 East 60th Street
Chicago, IL 60637, USA
t: +1 773 702 7700
f: +1 773-702-9756
e:sales@press.uchicago.edu
www.press.uchicago.edu

© Bristol University Press 2019

British Library Cataloguing in Publication Data
A catalogue record for this book is available from the British Library.

Library of Congress Cataloging-in-Publication Data
A catalog record for this book has been requested.

ISBN 978-1-5292-0225-0 paperback
ISBN 978-1-5292-0226-7 ePub
ISBN 978-1-5292-0228-1 Mobi
ISBN 978-1-5292-0227-4 ePdf

The right of Jefferson Frank, Norman Gowar and Michael Naef to be identified
as authors of this work has been asserted by them in accordance with the 1988
Copyright, Designs and Patents Act.

Cover design by blu inc, Bristol

Front cover: image kindly supplied by iStock
Printed and bound in Great Britain by CMP, Poole
Bristol University Press uses environmentally responsible print partners

To Judy Gowar (Greene), who
always got the important
things right.

Contents

List of Figures

List of Tables

Notes on the Authors

Jefferson Frank was founding head of the Economics Department at Royal Holloway, University of London. Trained at Yale as a macroeconomist, Jeff has also extensively investigated the gender pay gap, BME and LGBTQ discrimination in the wider economy and in the university sector. He is the author of *The Responsible Economy* (Routledge, 2014) where he explores the interactions between ethical behaviour and economic efficiency. Jeff's current research is focussed upon public policy and the millennials, using focus groups to explore the policy objectives of millennials. He is researching how monetary and macroeconomic policy has impacted upon the millennial generation. Jeff has been Visiting Professor at Berkeley and Harvard universities and he is a Fellow of the Academy of Social Sciences.

Norman Gowar, Professor Emeritus of Mathematics at the University of London, is a former Principal of Royal Holloway. He was a founder member of the Open University and a major contributor to its first suite of mathematics courses and to its development during two terms as Pro-Vice Chancellor responsible for planning and resource allocation. After setting up a Centre for Mathematics Education, he went on to become Deputy Vice Chancellor before joining Royal Holloway in 1990 from which he retired in 2000. He led the consultation on the introduction of the Office of the Independent Adjudicator for Student Complaints and as its first Chairman oversaw its establishment and first six years of operation.

Michael Naef is Reader in Economics at Royal Holloway, University of London. Educated in Zurich at a time when creative and progressive economic thought was flourishing, he has pursued a number of research interests around the question of what drives people to make the choices they do. Traditional economics assumes self-interest as the only and all-powerful motivator. Michael has contributed to widening the scope of what may interest economists to include a great number of 'soft' factors that have surprisingly profound impacts on people's choices. Lately he has branched out into investigations of weird and wonderful substances (testosterone, estrogen, sulpiride), examining the interface between material biological effects and models of economic behaviour. He has published widely, including in *Nature* and the *American Economic Review*.

Preface

There has been a lot of press coverage about the current crisis in English universities, ranging from extremely high Vice Chancellor salaries to commensurately high indebtedness of our students. The government is currently holding a review of post-18 education with a view to 'driving up quality, increasing choice and ensuring value for money'.

There has been a major strike by the University and College Union. While occasioned by specific employer proposals to end the defined benefits pension scheme, there was a broader background of alienation. In this environment, there needs to be a healing process. We see this book as part of that process. We hope that the reader does not see us as attacking anyone and that policy makers and the higher education sector engage with the ideas we express here.

Higher education has been one of the few areas of the public sector that has been isolated from austerity and indeed has seen significant increases in taxpayer support, albeit not widely advertised. In other research, we are studying generational inequality. Universities are an example where millennials and the following generation gain immediate benefit from expenditure, but it remains the case that they will be repaying not only their individual student debts but also general government debt taken out to pay the up-front subsidies in the student loan system. They are entitled to see that we spend their money wisely.

Our interest is in designing mechanisms that efficiently achieve desired outcomes. Everyone states that they want high quality education with widening participation. The increase in fees and the contingent loan system, based upon the Browne Report, was intended to bring about those results. That the marketisation of higher education hasn't achieved these objectives means either that it is an inappropriate venture or that there are flaws in the design of the mechanism. Others have commented extensively on the limits to markets in education. Our job in this book is to identify the design flaws in the attempts at marketization and propose remedies. We come to this task with some strong beliefs and principles. We believe in academic freedom for lecturers and students, and that there should be diverse voices engaging in reasoned debate on university campuses throughout the country. It is also our belief that students benefit from programmes in literature and the arts, in modern languages, just as much as they benefit from studying mathematics and economics. Students in the sciences need a hinterland in the humanities and those in the humanities need an understanding of scientific method if they are to apply their resources to the issues confronting society.

Money, employability and all those things are not the measure of an economic system. The citizens – through their elected government – determine the values by which economic outcomes can be measured. This can be the number of cars in the driveway, but it can be access to public libraries and parks, or it can be the social environment in the country. In this book, we take the objectives of the citizens and their government of the day as being precisely what the government states for universities. Free speech, quality of education, value for money and widening participation. We want to see put in place efficient mechanisms to achieve those goals.

In an ideal world, we believe that there are strong arguments to support the view that university education should be free. An educated society contains its own value, and pricing education devalues the experience. However, we recognise that the current view is to keep tax rates low and in that context health and pre-university education have a higher priority. Our approach therefore is to work within the principles laid down in the Browne Report but to demonstrate remediable weaknesses in their implementation.

As a final note, however, we think it important to bring back the enthusiasm and excitement that characterised – for example – the new universities in the 1960s and 1970s. Any organisation or sector works best with that positive environment. Our ideas are designed to set each institution free to aim to be the best in its chosen endeavours. This will be different for each university or other higher education provider. We include private providers in this diversity, and give the context and the regulation that allows for efficient private provision in some areas of the sector. We see diversity in mission across institutions as adding to the sector in the same way as we advise students to seek out their own goals, determine how to balance their strengths and interests, and pursue their life course as an individual and with enthusiasm.

1

Introduction

The National Audit Office issued its report on 'The higher education market' in December 2017.[1] This identifies that, despite a 50 per cent increase in upfront public funding for teaching, only 32 per cent of students believe that they are receiving value for money. The extension of higher education throughout less advantaged backgrounds is weak and concentrated in the less prestigious universities. There is little price competition and little financial reward for rising in the league tables. In introducing the new Office for Students (OfS) in the 2017 Higher Education and Research Act, the government noted the rampant grade inflation in degree classifications. Recently, there has been a sharp increase in 'unconditional offers' to 23 per cent of university applicants. The Higher Education minister is quoted as saying that this 'undermines the credibility of the university system' (BBC News, 26 July 2018). The new Office for Students is charged to: maintain autonomy of higher education providers; promote quality; encourage competition; promote value for money; and promote equality of opportunity.

The Labour Party promise, in its 2017 General Election Manifesto, to eliminate student fees is generally viewed as a significant political success. The Party gained seats, particularly in constituencies with high university student populations. Arguably in consequence, the government has instituted a Review of Post-18 Education and Funding to conclude in early 2019. This Review in particular maintains the principles of income-contingent contributions by students to education costs and the absence of a cap on post-18 education. It is presumed that the wording of both principles is carefully chosen to allow for significant changes to the current funding regime. Notably, the 'absence of a cap on post-18 education' need not imply the 'absence of a cap on university students'. Students can instead follow their interests into first rate apprenticeships and technical programmes. While awaiting the findings of the Review, the government has already capped tuition fees from rising further and made the repayments on student loans less onerous.

As if all that wasn't enough, academics went on strike in 2018 over proposed draconian cuts to the pension system. Despite the 50 per cent increase in upfront public funding for teaching, the employers' organisation (Universities UK) was unwilling to cover the projected shortfall in the scheme with increased contributions (on the 2/3, 1/3 share between universities and academics that had previously been agreed). The pensions issue has not been resolved and is likely to colour the campus environment for some time to come. It is in fact part of a broader malaise wherein senior managements and academics seem to have lost grasp of having a common purpose. Academics complain of 'managerialism', 'consumerism' and now – more darkly and troublesome – a serious threat to academic freedom.

The extraordinary thing about the 'crisis in English universities' is that – unlike much of the public sector – it is not a result of cost-cutting during austerity. Universities are one of the few areas where funding has substantially increased. Indeed, the malaise affecting universities seems akin to the woes that can befall an unprepared lottery winner who was, in fact, reasonably happy in their existing life. In a burst of excitement, the lottery winner quits their job and buys a footballer's house. Their relatives come by demanding their share of the winnings and they are besieged by financial experts with brilliant ideas for making even more money. Major lotteries offer the winners advice on how to keep control of their lives and to avoid losing perspective. A bit belatedly, we are putting into the pot some ideas for the sector and the government.

The higher education market

Prior to the 2011 reforms, British universities were a centuries-long success story. The international reputation of our universities was high, with students from around the world coming here to study. If it wasn't broke, why fix it?

Other commentators have discussed why viewing higher education as a market, and students as consumers, can be damaging in itself. Although we have considerable sympathy for that view, we feel that both sides of that debate have made their points. The primary purpose of this book is to take on the market policies on their own terms. The market is badly designed and has consequently led to poor value for money and a lowered quality of education. There are three main features of the market that are problematic:

1. The uncapping of student numbers, at the institution and sector level, has severely diminished competition. Rather than engaging in expensive and difficult competition, universities can simply admit weaker students.
2. The maximum fee (which, in practice, has become the universal fee) of £9000 was set too high, so that there is no need for universities to be efficient.
3. The contingent repayment loan system rewards failure by subsidising poor performance on poorly designed degrees.

The Browne Report (2010) proposed that student numbers be set over the sector, so that universities had to compete for this fixed number of students.[2] Instead, student numbers were uncapped, at a stroke eliminating competition. The top universities have dramatically expanded their student numbers. The next tier in the hierarchy have not competed for the top students, but have gone down the demand curve, and so on through the hierarchy.

Browne essentially proposed fees of £6000, roughly the cost of education per student, and the government expected fees to average £7500. Fees of £9000 have simply left the sector awash with funds, with little need to achieve efficiency in their use. Even a completely hapless management would run a surplus in this environment.

Student loans incur a high interest rate of RPI plus 3 per cent, currently totalling 6.1 per cent, while studying and – after graduation – for incomes over £45,000. Because of this high interest rate, and fees set above the cost of education, a financially successful student (earning more than £45,000) is not only not subsidised, but pays for subsidies to other students. The subsidisation of student loans occurs as students who consistently earn below the threshold (currently £25,000) eventually have the balance of their loans written off. The government anticipates writing off up to 50 per cent of the loans provided. The extreme skewness of the contingent-repayment loan system and high write-off rate rewards failure.

As a further irony, the marketisation of higher education is not extended to academic pay and conditions. Lord Stern's report (2016) on the Research Excellence Framework (REF) proposed measures to cut the transfer market for academics, which was driving up academic salaries.[3] These measures have been partially adopted for the 2021 REF, and are planned to be adopted in full for the subsequent REF. Why should universities compete for students, but not for academics?

The grade inflation endemic in the current system arises in part from the withering away of an effective external examiner system. The remuneration for externals, however, has become derisory at levels little changed from the 1970s. Traditionally, it was goodwill and professional commitment on the part of academics that meant that the rates of pay did not matter. If the current 'managerialism' in universities wants to emphasise performance management of academics, however, it has to understand that things previously provided from goodwill will in the future have to be remunerated.

Some simple arithmetic

There is a simple arithmetic of university costs. If the average academic pay is £60,000 a year (including some overheads), the student–staff ratio (SSR) is 20 to 1, and academic salaries represent the traditional 50 per cent of university teaching budgets, then the cost per student is £6,000. This implicit arithmetic was the basis of the Browne Report's proposal for fees of roughly that level, which also coincided with existing funding. The extent to which the SSR is lower in some universities reflects other income, from research, for example.

This level of costs is a bargain compared to fee levels in Australia, North America and other countries, and is perhaps based on SSRs that are too high. A strong argument can be made that English universities have been a success story of remarkable productivity and efficiency, by international standards. Evidence for this is the large number of overseas students who attend English universities, paying significantly higher fees (nearly double or more) than Home and European Union (HEU) students, although post Brexit these figures are looking less robust.

The simple arithmetic means that the new flows of funds into universities – turning into a flood by the time all cohorts were paying the higher fees of £9000 and student numbers were uncapped – had to go into one of three broad categories. The first possibility is academic salaries. However, the public sector pay cap meant that academic salaries were largely frozen. In real terms, as in seen in Figure 1.1, they have fallen substantially since the academic year 2010/11, rather than rising. Although we only have data for non-academic staff from a later date, increases for this group as a whole were also contained.

Figure 1.1: Average real salary: academic and non-academic staff

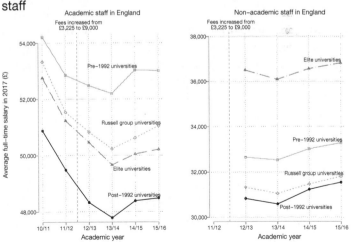

Source: Annual Salary Survey, *Times Higher Education* 2012–17 (usually published in a late Spring edition).

In this book, to clarify and simplify discussion we distinguish between four groupings of universities: elite (Cambridge, Imperial, Oxford, the LSE, UCL); the Russell Group; the pre-1992 universities; and the post-1992 universities. In dividing institutions into the four groups we are simply reflecting the reality of current funding and reputation. It is useful for analysis and to understand what is happening throughout the sector. The elite universities, for example, have much more income and expenditure per student than do other universities. This does not mean that they are more 'important' than other institutions. We will argue throughout the book that each institution needs to find its own niche and to achieve excellence in its chosen mission.

The next possibility is to hire new academics to lower the SSR. The English university system harks back to the Oxbridge model of small tutorials and frequent interactions between academic staff and students. Financial realities, as the system expanded without commensurate funding increases, have moved us away from that educational approach. A natural use of the new funds would have been to restore more intensive teaching. Students could benefit from smaller classes and personal advisors who actually know the student and can write reference letters that say more than repeat the student's transcript. There could be course projects and final year dissertations with significant discussions between tutor and student. This would be consistent with students paying high fees and expecting an improvement in the teaching environment.

The final option is the broad category of 'other expenditures'. This can be more administrators and higher Vice Chancellor pay, as now reported regularly in the press. It can also be new Sports and Student Centres, shopping malls and new student housing. While academics would put the academic–student interaction at the heart of the university, well-functioning administrative support and good auxiliary facilities have value. We will however later discuss why the subject department is at the heart of a successful university. This means that the most effective administration is typically at the coalface, departmental level. Good laboratories and classrooms have real value, but must be planned and built with academics playing a full, determinative role in design and take precedence over facilities designed to attract students rather than teach them.

Figure 1.2: University expenditure percentages

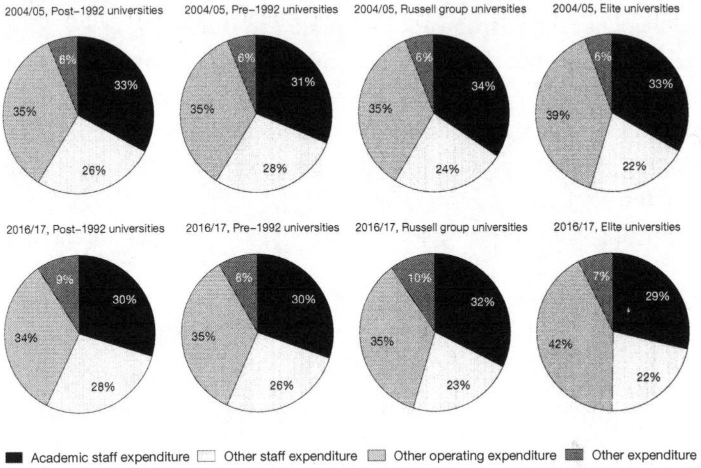

2004/05, Post–1992 universities   2004/05, Pre–1992 universities   2004/05, Russell group universities   2004/05, Elite universities

2016/17, Post–1992 universities   2016/17, Pre–1992 universities   2016/17, Russell group universities   2016/17, Elite universities

■ Academic staff expenditure ☐ Other staff expenditure ▨ Other operating expenditure ■ Other expenditure

Note: HE institutions with fewer than ten students are excluded in this figure.

Source: HESA Finance Record 2004/05 and 2016/17

Figure 1.2 shows that all four university groups have similar expenditure shares (about 30 per cent of total expenditures) for academic staff. Further, this has declined by a few percentage points between 2004/05 and 2016/17. While the percentage declines might seem small, it reflects a large sum of expenditure in pounds transferred from academic staffing to 'other expenditures'. What certainly has not happened is a large increase in academic staffing to substantially lower the SSR.

This book is about ideas and concepts. We will be taking a large chisel to the current structure of university funding and fees, rather than being engaged in fine detail work. As such, we will adopt simple approximate numbers for our discussion throughout the book: core costs of teaching are the £6000 identified by Browne; the current fees are £9000; and the current forecast repayment rate on student loans will be 50 per cent. That we are approximating these figures helps hugely in keeping our arithmetic simple, but is at little cost to our argument. Our points would not change if we more accurately wrote current fees of £9250, and so on.

The approximations do make for simple arithmetic when we come to proposals. For example, consider a proposal to lower fees to £6000 as a general level from the current £9000 (using our approximations). With the assumed current 50 per cent non-repayment rate, that lowers fee funding to universities by £3000 per head, but saves the taxpayer £1500 per student (the 50 per cent non-repayment on the £3000 reduction). We can come up with proposals on how to feed back those funds for improvements in the quality of education and widening participation, without making any further claims on the taxpayer.

Universities and airlines

When markets were being introduced into universities in England, there were concerns about the consumers – students – being sufficiently informed to make wise decisions. The proposed market raised similar problems to the privatisation of medicine. The information problems in medicine are immense. Since the doctor, not the patient, is better able to diagnose any ailments, it makes little sense to allow the patient to choose a heart operation over pharmaceuticals, or vice versa. Decisions have to be delegated from the patient to doctors, but the doctor has to have the right incentives to put the patient first. We have recently seen a crisis in the prescription of opioids, particularly in the US, that has possibly been supported by the wrong incentives facing pharmaceutical companies and the medical professionals.

Choosing one degree over another, or one university over another, is not really a life or death decision. If students apply themselves to their studies, they will do well whether they are at Oxford or at a lower-ranked university. The choice, however, is essentially once-off and a poor decision is difficult to rectify. In some ways, the information problems facing students are even more complex than those in medicine. Choices are more individualised. It is the student who knows how they feel about studying English Literature as against Accounting. Compounding that, students have been subjected to extremely poor advice. Less privileged students have been steered to lower ranked universities and not to Oxbridge. They have been steered to Business Studies degrees rather than Mathematics and Physics, on the basis of simplistic views about employability.

Ironically, having ignored these information arguments against marketisation, the authorities have been moving us to the worst of both worlds by micromanagement. On the basis that students do not have the information for markets to work, large sums are being spent on creating information. We feel that the NSS (National Student Survey) and the bulk of work of the QAA (Quality Assurance Agency), including the TEF (Teaching Excellence Framework) is a waste of taxpayer and student money, simply because the information produced is not the pertinent information.

We feel that the primary interest of the taxpayer, in return for their large subsidies to higher education, is that the legitimacy and the 'safety' of the product is ensured. In particular, the government should ensure the integrity of degrees awarded. It is now not unusual for a mid-ranked university to be offering 1/3 or more first-class degrees. This rise has coincided with the policy changes. The taxpayer and the student are entitled to have degrees that properly assure the public that the student has the requisite qualifications of that degree. The QAA has taken on the issue of the external examination system, but is adopting the approach of benchmarking degrees and subjects, with a view to training external examiners. We simply don't accept that an experienced senior academic does not know what is involved in a university degree, or what constitutes the important components of a degree in their subject. The problem is that the primacy of senior externals has been watered down, partly through the lack of remuneration, and partly through weakening of the input and independence of the external under pressure to award more firsts.

We view efficient regulation of higher education as analogous to air travel. The primary function of the government is to ensure that travel is safe. Private airlines will simply not have the full incentive to maintain planes to zero tolerance. If a crash occurs due to poor maintenance or a poorly-trained pilot, the airline simply goes bankrupt. It is the government that must ensure that planes are maintained and pilots must meet strict standards of training and professionalism. In the same way, the primary function of university regulation must be to maintain the integrity of degrees and assessment.

In addition, airlines cannot be allowed to arbitrarily decide where to take off and land, what routes to fly and with what frequency. This is partially an issue of air traffic control, but also an issue of externalities and the nature of competition. Airspace is in limited supply and there are potential congestion externalities. In an uncontrolled market, there is the danger that there will be frequent flights from London to New York, but no convenient way of getting to Albuquerque. In the same way, the government can – through its arm's-length agency – determine student numbers at universities and across subjects. Otherwise, all universities may duplicate popular courses in Management and in Creative Writing, and no one will end up offering the currently unpopular Modern Languages or Literature.

Uncontrolled airline markets may have a problem about the quality of service in the sense of delayed or cancelled flights, or overbooking passengers on a flight. It is desirable and economically efficient for the authorities to be involved in ensuring that the passenger gets from point A to point B. In fact, the current European air compensation rules are largely efficient. If one is two hours late, one gets a certain level of compensation; three hours late, more; and so on. When volcanic ash over Iceland caused the cancellation of many flights, airlines complained that it wasn't 'fair' for them to pay compensation. It was however economically efficient in terms of airlines organising overnight stays for delayed passengers, finding an alternative way home as quickly as possible, and avoiding expensive litigation over whether or not the airline was at fault. 'The best is the enemy of the good' holds for economic policy as much as anywhere else. Along these lines, we see potential for greater recognition for the role of the Office of the Independent Adjudicator (OIA) in handling serious student complaints.

What a government does not have to do, and should not do, is regulate the quality of the food and entertainment on the airplane, or run surveys on these subjects. That information is readily learned by experience in flying, and by reading surveys on the internet. In the same way, using taxpayer funds for the NSS and the TEF simply borders on the bizarre. We think that the NSS and TEF simply measure the wrong things, analogous to the food service and not to true educational quality. Further, the TEF – with its gold, silver and bronze awards – de-emphasises the importance of fit to the student. The TEF, NSS, employability and other measures presume that one course is objectively better than another. Our vision of a higher education system, in contrast, is one where every institution is performing at a high standard for its chosen mission and should attract the students whose interests and qualifications best match the offerings.

The traditional ways of gathering information allow a focus upon the educational value of a course and its suitability for the student's particular strengths and interests. Students can collect this information from careers advisers in their school, from the internet, from talking to people they know who go to a particular university or take particular degrees, from visits to schools by university staff and – most important of all – by visiting the institution. Where there is a lack of information it primarily concerns students from less advantaged backgrounds and schools less attuned to directing students to the most appropriate universities. This is best tackled as a widening participation issue, however, and we will argue that the best way to do this is to incentivise individual universities to target these students.

There is a further sense in which the current market for students can be compared to airlines. Under the historical system of regulation, airlines faced a fixed price and competed on the quality of food service, free alcohol and eventually on-board entertainment systems. No one in the higher education sector was greatly surprised that the £9000 cap turned into a fixed £9000 fee across universities and programmes. As with price regulated airlines, universities are competing on peripherals such as student centres. The difference is that for universities the government and its agencies have failed to ensure safety in the sense that the integrity of degrees and the fundamental quality of teaching has been sacrificed to compete, at least in part, with grade inflation.

The hierarchy of airlines and of universities

Some North American universities have 'Honours' programmes where selected students can get a more intensive education of higher quality than the normal degree at the same university in the same subject. At English universities, this distinction is not currently very common, but may potentially arise as a way to resolve some of the current dilemmas in universities. This is not dissimilar to the idea, once more common, of a general degree and single honours degree. The first may allow for a wide selection of courses, the second a more focused programme with requirements for some courses at the highest level. Both have value but they are different. If grade inflation means that the standard degree at a good mid-range university is no longer an entry into jobs at top firms, introducing a more rigorous degree may serve the purpose. Somewhat more indirectly, the degree subject may still allow that university to certify some of its students at a higher level. A first-class degree in theoretical physics may qualify the student for an entry post at a major accounting and consultancy firm, even if a first-class on the accounting degree at that same university does not.

Looking at airlines, what stands out is that there are a limited number of high quality (irrespective of class of travel) airlines that persist in the rankings from year-to-year: Emirates, Qatar, Singapore, Cathay Pacific, All Nippon Airways, Air New Zealand, and a few others. The next tier of airlines has shown a downward slide in their ratings. United Airlines suffered extremely bad publicity when a passenger was dragged off the plane. British Airways moved from a business model with free meals in all classes to one where the passenger could buy Marks & Spencer's sandwiches. The budget airlines, notably Ryanair, continued with a provocative expression of being low-cost.

This sort of hierarchy has always existed in universities. As we will discuss later, this is in part due to network externalities. Looking at the research side of the university, a department with top researchers attracts more top researchers. In the same way, having good students attracts more good students. We will explore how the new market system at universities has entrenched and expanded the existing hierarchy of universities, and how the particularly challenged universities are those in the middle.

As we have said, we distinguish between elite universities, the Russell Group, the pre-1992 non-Russell universities and the post-1992 universities. That these universities form distinct classes in a hierarchy can be seen from their income levels (see Figure 1.3).

This income includes all the research and other income obtained by the university, and therefore differs from the funds available for teaching. Nonetheless, it is pertinent that the elite universities have about £60,000 in income per student and the

Figure 1.3: Total income per student

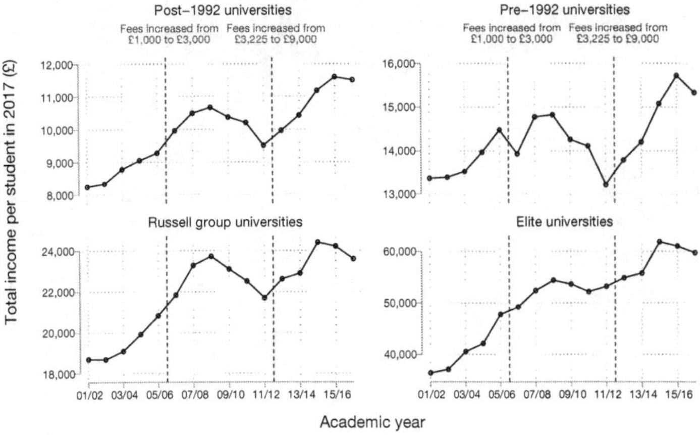

Note: HE institutions with fewer than ten students are excluded in this figure.

Source: HESA Finance and Student Record 2001/02–2016/17

post-1992 universities only about £11,500. It can also be seen that income went up sharply at all classes of university with the increase in fees and uncapped student numbers.

With uncontrolled numbers and high fees, the top universities had an incentive to attract more students overall and expand dramatically. Figure 1.4 looks at overall numbers and Figure 1.5 undergraduate numbers. Other pre- and post-1992 universities, lower down in the pecking order, first suffered a fall in overall numbers but have subsequently recovered. With respect to undergraduate numbers, the post-1992 remain below their peak.

A more accurate picture of the direct effects of the new funding and fees regime, however, is given by concentrating upon UK-domiciled students, as shown in Figure 1.6. Looking at UK students, the elite and Russell Group universities have hugely expanded at the expense of both pre- and post-1992 universities. These universities remain well below their pre-increase UK student numbers.

We make two additional points on student numbers. Looking at non-UK students, the numbers from the EU and from other locations was relatively stable at the pre- and post-1992 universities, with substantial increases at the elite and Russell universities. The

Figure 1.4: Student numbers overall

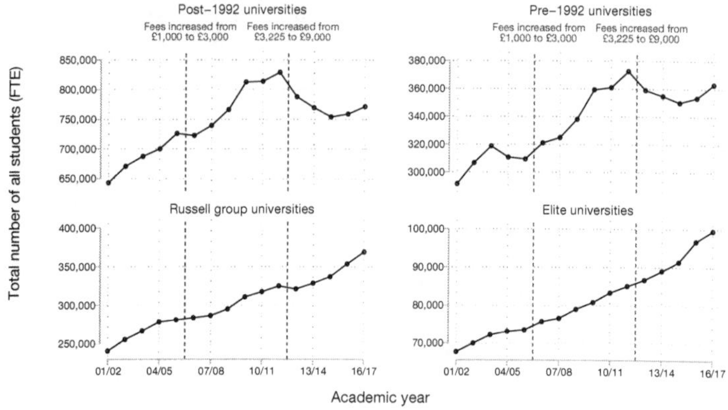

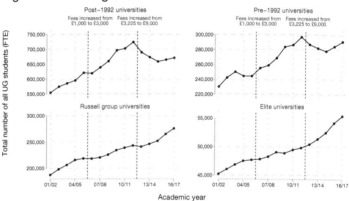

Source: HESA Student Record 2001/02–2016/17

Figure 1.5: Undergraduate student numbers

Source: HESA Student Record 2001/02–2016/17

Brexit effect will appear after these dates, but in any case, the number of EU students (as opposed to staff) is relatively low (see Figure 1.7).

The expansion envisaged by Browne was intended to widen participation by non-traditional groups, with more students entering university from lower income households and from BME backgrounds. The intention was that the student intake at Oxford would reflect the state–private ratio in the country, and not be disproportionately filled with better-off privately-educated students.

Figure 1.6: UK student numbers

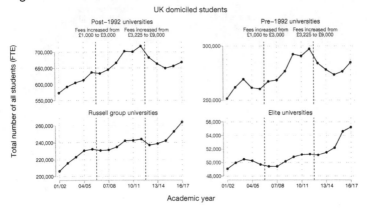

Source: HESA Student Record 2001/02–2016/17

Figure 1.7: Student numbers EU and other

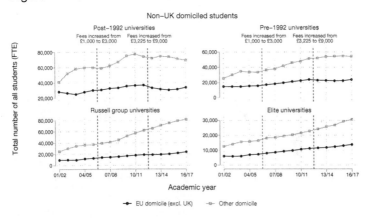

Source: HESA Student Record 2001/02–2016/17

The middle-class Russell Group and pre-1992 universities would similarly broaden their intake.

Looking at percentages of state school students, the figures do show some limited improvement at the top universities, from a relatively low base (see Figure 1.8).

Figure 1.8: Participation by state school students

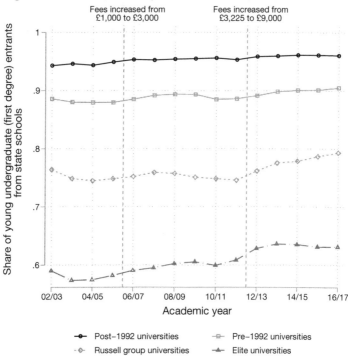

Source: HESA Student Record 2002/03–2016/17

Figure 1.9 shows a noticeable decline in the percentage of undergraduates of white ethnicity. When we break up the entrants by ethnicity in Figure 1.10, we find however that the predominant increases in participation are among students of Asian ethnicity – black students remain severely under-represented at the top universities. In Table 1.1, we show the distribution of students of a given ethnicity across the four groups of universities. For students of Asian ethnicity, 5 per cent attend the elite universities, roughly comparable to the 3 per cent of white students who attend. Only 1 per cent of black students attend these universities. Black students are similarly underrepresented at the Russell Group universities and overrepresented at the post-1992 universities.

Figure 1.9: Participation by ethnicity: white

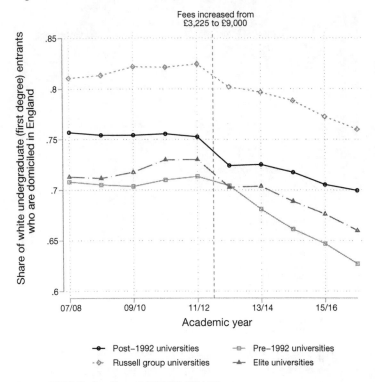

Source: HESA Student Record 2007/08–2016/17

Figure 1.10: Participation by ethnic background

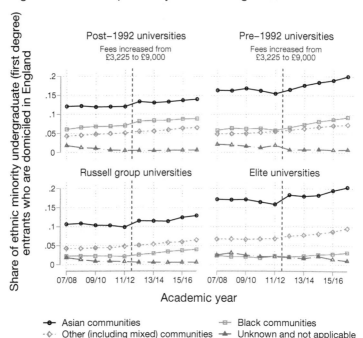

Source: HESA Student Record 2007/08–2016/17

Table 1.1: University type attended by each ethnicity

	Asian communities	Black communities	White communities
Elite universities	5%	1%	3%
Russell group universities	19%	12%	25%
Pre-1992 universities	26%	24%	18%
Post-1992 universities	50%	63%	54%

Source: HESA Student Record 2016/17

A further measure of widening participation is to look at neighbourhoods with traditionally low participation rates (see Figure 1.11). This shows little progress among the elite universities, and only modest improvements for the Russell and pre-1992 universities. Widening participation ultimately entails that each university looks more like England as a whole, with representative diversity reflecting the ethnic and social background of students. It is clear that the best funded universities have much more to do in this regard.

We have emphasised that each university should define its own mission and achieve excellence in its chosen sphere of activities. The government has been surprised that each university has by and large chosen to set fees at the maximum allowed level. In principle, there is nothing wrong with a fixed price across comparable courses,

Figure 1.11: Participation by neighbourhood

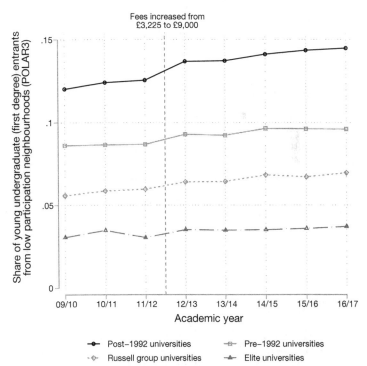

Source: HESA Student Record 2009/10–2016/17

if the market is structured so that integrity is protected and the competition is over quality of education. Arguably, the now defunct Retail Price Maintenance for books preserved high service local and independent bookshops.

We will however argue that there is a role for different types of post-18 institutions, with different objectives, with different fee levels. Having different institutions serving different aspects of tertiary education, with different missions, is a good thing and reflects the different motivations and abilities of different students. What is inefficient is to have the same price for a high-cost institution where international researchers teach in small tutorials, and for a low-cost institution which is not as research-intensive. We will therefore propose a route for some institutions, which may have excellent teaching staff and programmes, to offer lower fees in return for a restoration of some of the block teaching grant.

This needs to avoid two potential problems, however. Every part of the system should be seeking to achieve excellence in its mission. Historically, the polytechnics filled an important niche in the overall system, as did the Open University, night schools such as Birkbeck College and, at a different level, the further education colleges. Private providers can also – as in the US – fill a niche in career-oriented programmes. We consider it a mistake to have every institution try to be UCL, but to imitate that institution less and less effectively as one moved down a hierarchy. The other problem is that we do not want widening participation to be an exercise where students from non-traditional backgrounds, for that reason alone, move into universities lower in the hierarchy. We want the ethnic and socio-economic diversity of this country to be reflected in every university.

Principles of a good system

For this book, we take the objectives for tertiary education to be those in the Higher Education and Research Act 2017: maintain autonomy of higher education providers; promote quality; encourage competition; promote value for money; and promote equality of opportunity.

The issue is to design markets and mechanisms that achieve those ends. We adopt the principles of good policies:

1. Do not micro-manage, but maintain the autonomy of providers. The funding agency should ensure the validity of degrees and the classification of results, should coordinate numbers of students and the incentive structure facing universities, but should then get out of the way and let each institution choose its own path towards excellence.
2. Competition is not of value in its own right, but in terms of what it can help achieve. The system should encourage universities to compete for the best students appropriate for their programmes by developing the best programmes to meet their chosen market niche.
3. The system set up should ensure that students from all backgrounds choose the most appropriate programme for themselves irrespective of financial costs, either at university or in other forms of post-secondary education and training, and should set up incentives such that institutions actively seek out students of all backgrounds to achieve a diverse student mix.
4. The system should make good economic sense for the student and the general taxpayer.

There is no free lunch

We will come to specific policy proposals in the final chapter, after we have explored the specifics of where we are now, what mechanisms are likely to work and which will be inefficient. In an ideal world, we would like to be able to lower fees to students, raise potential income for universities and maintain the taxpayer contribution at its current level. It may well be the case that more efficient organisation of university funding and fees will allow that to happen, but efficiency gains should prudently not be banked until they actually occur in practice. For that reason, the balance between lowering student fees − along with the associated costs of attending university such as accommodation − and its impact on funding for universities will remain a political decision. We can help construct the budget line that defines the trade-offs in an efficient organisation of higher education funding and fees, but ultimately the government will have to choose how much goes to universities in funding and the division of that amount between students and the taxpayer.

Universities have just had, from 2011 to 2018, the 'seven fat years' of abundance, and – even under neutral government policies – will be entering the 'seven lean years'. The number of 18-year-olds will continue to decline in the immediate future, although a recent report by the Higher Education Policy Institute[4] observes that the demographics of the number of 18-year-olds will recover in the 2020s. However, that eventual increase in numbers is mixed news since it means that the total funding bill facing government will rise without offsetting measures in cutting fees. Further, there is the shadow of Brexit and the implications for EU and indeed all overseas students. England may be less attractive for Chinese and other students if we are no longer part of the European Union. The 'public sector pay cap' is being lifted and it is to be expected that academic salaries will start to rise significantly. Dealing conclusively with the projected deficit in the USS pension scheme may require employer contributions to rise by up to 7 per cent of the relevant salary bill.

None of this is insurmountable. British universities were in a strong position in 2011 when the current schemes came into play and – leaving aside self-inflicted wounds such as the ongoing disputes between the employers (Universities UK) and their academic staff through the recognised trade union (University and College Union) – there is no reason why things cannot be put back on track again. We hope that this book helps in that process.

The plan of the book

Chapter Two considers the development of the university system and the background to the current policies and the various reviews conducted at different points in time. The 1963 Robbins Report and the 1997 Dearing Report in many ways followed a consistent vision of what universities were all about and how participation could best be expanded to meet the needs of a technological society. Even though it is much more about financial structure and market mechanisms than about philosophy, it is not clear that the 2010 Browne Report meant to substantially change the nature of university education. In any case, Scotland has adopted a different set of policies based upon free fees. We conclude with a Short Note examining the Scottish approach and provide arguments for subsidisation of fees and even free fees, if affordable at some future date.

Chapter Three develops our model of 'markets without competition'. Before Browne, each university had a student number target. Universities competed not for the number of students, but to try to attract the best students. Browne proposed a sector-wide limit on the number of students, so again universities would have to compete with each other for students. It would make sense to compete for the best students. By removing the cap on student numbers, the government killed competition with a stroke – universities could simply move down the demand curve and admit weaker students. Both to attract these students – and sometimes by necessity to ensure that they progressed in their degrees – grade inflation was a natural result.

Chapter Four considers how resources are allocated in a 'not for profit' organisation across the various stakeholders. If a university has an overall stringent budget, it cannot be too inefficient or it will run the risk of bankruptcy. But, with generous funding, as with the current allocations, funds can be adopted to meet the preferences of stakeholders, corresponding to their power in decision-making. We examine the negative results from current 'managerialism' in universities and consider how to restore a balance in governance and in the role of academics in the years to come. An important part of this is valuing students not only today, but in the future as alumni and donors.

Chapter Five explores the institutions that can help to ensure quality. We emphasise the external examining system in ensuring the credibility of degrees, and express reservations over the emphasis of the QAA upon the TEF and the NSS. We look at the SSR as the measure of inputs into the educational process, and consider the limits to sustainability of the current approaches by universities and the regulatory agencies.

Chapter Six looks at widening participation and student loans. The BME percentage, and participation by students from lower income households, has grown to a modest extent across university classes. Top universities are lagging in this area. Currently, the Office for Fair Access (OFFA) seeks statements of bureaucratic process rather than setting enforced targets. We consider how the student loan scheme currently rewards failure. Widening participation is in part about making all of our universities representative of the population of the country as a whole. But it is also about providing a diversity of institutions so that all – whatever their age or educational and social background – receive support in their life endeavours. The Open University was a distinctly British solution to some of the issues of access and lifelong learning, and we consider in a Short Note the history of the OU and how its distinctiveness might be maintained. It is a way of offering a lower cost education, but one that is specifically tailored to be first rate at what it does with a reliable and recognised standard of qualifications. We also consider the potential for private providers, drawing upon the US experience. We deliberately put this issue in a Short Note to our discussion on widening participation, since the US system works in providing vocational entry for students who would otherwise be totally left behind. For-profit institutions in the US and potentially in the UK are not an effective route to providing traditional degrees in a context where we want competition to be about quality and not just degree certificates.

Chapter Seven considers the role for different institutions in the future and brings together our policy recommendations. A system where everyone tries to do the same thing, and some are very good at it and some are not very good at it, is inefficient. Universities should specialise. We show why the current funding system has led to greater dominance of hierarchical rankings and groups (such as the Russell Group). Centralised systems to inform students such as league tables have led to uniformity of mission rather than meeting the professed need for greater diversity. This can only be undone by universities finding their individual niche and excelling in their niche. For some universities, this means a focus on teaching, and we discuss how they might choose a different funding regime. But for the entire sector, we propose to set up mechanisms and incentives that offer what the government claimed for the funding regime, and what the sector claims it wants – free speech, autonomy of institutions, real quality competition, value for money and equality of opportunity.

2

How Did We Get Here?

The primary purpose of this book is to analyse the effects of recent policy decisions to attempt to introduce a market and competition into the university system in the belief that this will increase quality and reduce costs. Given the introduction of student fees as the overwhelming source of funding, it is a presumed consequence that students will increasingly ask questions about value for money. Students are leaving university with up to £60,000 in debt, at a punitive interest rate of up to 6.3 per cent. This will affect their ability to gain a foothold on the housing ladder, or other of the common rites of passage accessed by previous generations. It potentially limits labour market flexibility, both because graduates will not be able to afford to live in some areas of the country but also because they may make career choices limited by their debts.

Before we turn to these issues, this chapter is an attempt to sketch a brief description of historic changes in Higher Education policy and indicate the direction of travel that has led us to where we are. The emphasis will be on universities in England since the policies adopted elsewhere in the UK have recently differed. Scotland under devolution has taken the approach of maintaining free fees, as we discuss at the end of this chapter. This survey is by no means intended to be comprehensive, but an indication of policy issues that have culminated in those which are the main subject of our analysis.

Until the 1830s Oxford and Cambridge were the only universities in England. Early in the nineteenth century a number of medical schools and 'mechanical institutes' developed. These relied on private financial support from individuals and local business and were poorly funded compared to Oxford and Cambridge which had ancient endowments and a wealthy clientele. In London, the 'London University' and King's College were established in 1826 and 1829 respectively, but without degree awarding powers. The funding for these new colleges came partly from an increasing concern for moral obligations to the underprivileged and partly for the need to enhance the nation's capacity for medical, scientific and technical advance. This need was perceived also at government level by the advances in Germany in particular which was seen as a major economic and political threat. All attempts to give these institutions university status and degree awarding powers were fought off by Oxford and Cambridge.

In 1832, the University of Durham was established by Act of Parliament with degree awarding powers after an agreement that final examinations would be subject to oversight of external examiners from Oxford. In 1836, the University of London was established with degree awarding powers and the 'London university' became University College London, which together with King's became colleges of the new university. In 1840, the University of London opened its doors to students other than those from UCL and King's and awarded degrees to any man who could pass the examination. In 1878, it opened these same opportunities to women. Oxford and Cambridge awarded degrees only to members of the Anglican church (although others could be students and take the examinations). This restriction did not apply to the University of London and so its establishment was a significant watershed. During the second half of the nineteenth century the number of colleges increased across the country and played an important role in preparing students for the examinations of the University of London, which effectively became an examinations and degree awarding body with its own constituent colleges driving the curriculum and standards and with students from outside the university being awarded 'external' degrees. A number of new constituent colleges of the university were established in London including two colleges exclusively for women. In 1900, the University of London became a teaching university as well as an examining body and with its constituent colleges becoming in effect a federal university. At the beginning of the twentieth century many of the colleges outside London became universities in their own right: Birmingham, Manchester, Leeds, Liverpool, Bristol, Sheffield. (Newcastle became a partner with Durham and later independent.)

Universities in Germany were supported by the state. In response, in England government grants were introduced in 1889 together with scholarships for students. The number of these scholarships was augmented by local authorities and other benefactors and, by including a living allowance, helped widen the pool of those able to go to university. The importance of higher education was increasingly evident after the First World War and the level of government support gradually increased until a need was seen for a body to be established to advise government on the overall level of funding and to distribute it. To this end the University Grants Committee (UGC) was established in 1923. This committee was made up of experienced academics and shared the traditional values of universities as the pursuit of knowledge and understanding and passing this on to the next generation. It acted at arm's length from government and distanced government from the day-to-day running of universities.

The experience of the Second World War showed the vital importance of scientific and technical advance. This, together with the need for social changes exemplified by the Beveridge Report, fuelled the imperative to expand universities which had been set out in the report of the Anderson Committee. The UGC planned the establishment of eight new universities and this planning was brought to fruition by the Robbins Report.[1] It is interesting to recall the civilising principles by which Robbins conducted his enquiry. The Report set out its understanding of the purpose of higher education: 'to teach skills; to produce cultivated men and women; to maintain research in balance with teaching; and to promote common standards of citizenship'.

At the time of the Robbins Report (1963) 4 per cent of the cohort went to university (5.6 per cent of men and 2.5 per cent of women). There were other forms of higher education – full-time teacher training and further education and part-time provision, but in total only 15 per cent went on to some form of higher education. While at the time some argued that only this percentage of the population could cope with the demands of a university education, Robbins argued that the pool of talent would increase as the post-war reforms in school education bore fruit and declared that 'university places should be available to all who are qualified by ability and attainment to pursue them and wish to do so'. The Report ran to 335 pages, 178 recommendations and five volumes of research. All the recommendations were accepted and eight new universities established. Although fees were not abolished they were paid by the state on a means-tested basis, as were maintenance grants.

Similar expansion took place across Europe, again with free tuition. Unlike the European model, the English system was largely an expansion of the Oxbridge model of residential universities with all the concomitant expense of large campuses and student facilities. The University of London remained a notable exception, apart from Royal Holloway College, a residential college for women based in Surrey.

The expanded system continued to be overseen by the UGC and assumed no change to the nature and purpose of a university. Even in the areas of Science and Technology where some national priorities might by some have been thought to intervene, the mission of pure enquiry largely, but not exclusively dominated. (Government laboratories also pursued national objectives outside the university system.) It was clear that curiosity driven research often had striking and unforeseen practical pay-offs, sometimes years later, and the UGC protection of university autonomy played an important role. Security of academic tenure also reflected the importance of this spirit of independent enquiry and freedom from government interference. This was the case throughout Europe and had been reinforced by the experiences of the 1930s and by the US experience in the 1950s McCarthy era.

This expansion of universities from the mid-nineteenth century was paralleled by that of the polytechnics. These institutions responded more directly to the growing need for more technical, scientific and professional education and mirrored similar expansion on the continent. The polytechnic system became formalised by the establishment of the Council for National Academic Awards (CNAA) in 1965 which oversaw standards and awarded degrees. Funding was through local authorities (with funds provided on a formula basis by central government through the rate support grant). Standards were overseen by subject panels with membership drawn from universities, polytechnics and professional bodies. Polytechnics also offered sandwich courses on which periods of academic study were interlaced with industrial placements with students being paid by their employer during these periods. This not only helped influence the curriculum to meet the high-level needs of employers, but provided students with experience that meant they were well placed for future employment. The polytechnics also offered sub degree courses which were validated by the Business and Technology Education Council (BTEC). This was a valuable provision for those not wanting to pursue a full degree or not yet adequately prepared and added to that provided by higher education (HE) and further education (FE) colleges. It provided a recognised qualification but also a pathway to a full degree for those who showed the potential and wanted to follow that route. The polytechnics were an attractive option to conventional universities and their increasing popularity led to the establishment of a Polytechnic Central Admissions System.

The third strand of the higher education scene at this time was the Open University, established in 1969 with a Royal Charter enabling it to award its own degrees. This provided opportunities for adults to study on a part-time basis from home using centrally produced materials backed up by tutorials at local study centres and for some courses week-long summer schools. Materials were produced by a central core of academics augmented by colleagues from the universities and polytechnics where specialist contributions were sought. Likewise, tutors at study centres and summer schools were recruited from other parts of the system. For some students who had missed out on degree level study at 18 this provided an opportunity to take a full degree to train for a career change or to update themselves, others could take one-off courses as an educational enrichment for its own sake or to update or supplement their existing qualification. A fuller note on the Open University is given in Chapter Six. The Open University was an important element in widening participation and lifelong learning, and could continue to lead in those areas.

From the mid-1960s through the 1970s and 1980s there was a wide educational provision for higher education catering for all needs (as well as provision at FE level and through some universities' continuing education departments and through the Workers' Educational Association). Fees and means-tested maintenance grants were paid by the state, with better-off parents expected to top up to the levels provided to less well-off families. The Open University did charge fees in the low hundreds, with the university providing a fund to exempt students on low incomes. Although there was an understood pecking order for universities, a degree from a UK university was recognised worldwide as of an understood standard. For research, the number of Nobel prizes and citations belied the size of the population.

Government policy in the 1980s was dominated by a belief in the market, low taxation and responsibilities passing from the state to the individual. Grants to universities came under extreme pressure and the need was seen to be more selective in funding, particularly for research. The first (pilot) research selectivity exercise was introduced in 1985 under the auspices of the UGC. The intention was to create three levels of university: R, X, and T. R universities would be dominated by research (but retaining a teaching role). X universities would provide a balance between teaching and research along traditional lines. T universities would be teaching only, perhaps with some research conducted in personal time or through project funding but not through block grant. This was resisted strongly, mainly with the argument that a 'T university' was not a university as we know it.

The 1988 Education Reform Act transferred funding for fees and maintenance grants from Local Education Authorities to central government, partly because of considerable variability in the numbers and size of grants across the country. Maintenance grants were frozen at £2,265 (means tested with an additional £420 available as a loan to all students). Fees continued to be paid in full. Under the Act, the UGC was abolished in 1989 and replaced by the Universities Funding Council (UFC) whose remit conceded more influence to government over the allocations of grant. Separate arrangements were made for Scotland and Wales.

Partly in response to the universities' rejection of the idea of a 'T university' and partly consistent with attacks on local authorities, and pressure from some polytechnic directors, under the 1992 Further and Higher Education Act polytechnics were awarded university status and given the title of university with degree awarding powers. Funding of polytechnics was transferred from local authorities to central government under the aegis of the Higher Education Funding

Council for England (HEFCE) which replaced the UFC. We note here that, by severing links with local authorities, polytechnics became less sensitive to the needs of local communities and local business. The mission tended to drift away from the original purpose of these institutions. Some of these new universities had a long and distinguished history as polytechnics offering high standards and some excellent research in specific areas, while some had been upgraded to polytechnic status only recently. National oversight of standards for the former polytechnics was removed from the CNAA. Responsibility for further education and non-university higher education institutions remained under local authority control, but with changed arrangements for regulation. The task of custody of CNAA records and validation of courses in the non-university sector was taken on by the Open University under government contract.

The increasing pressure on funding during the 1980s and early 1990s and the search for extra income led to an increase in attention to attracting overseas students, whose numbers and fees were not capped by government. Maintenance grants for home students were converted to loans and there was increasing pressure from government to introduce fees but this was shot down by the backbenchers of the governing Conservative Party who saw it as a vote loser. The issue was kicked into touch by the establishment of the Dearing Committee.

It is interesting to compare the guiding principles it set itself to those of the Robbins Committee. The Dearing Report[2] set out the following principles:

The future will require higher education in the UK to:

- encourage and enable all students whether they demonstrate the highest intellectual potential or whether they have struggled to reach the threshold of higher education to achieve beyond their expectations;
- safeguard the rigour of its awards, ensuring that UK qualifications meet the needs of UK students and have standing throughout the world;

- be at the leading edge of world practice in effective learning and teaching;
- undertake research that matches the best in the world, and make its benefits available to the nation;
- ensure that its support for regional and local communities is at least comparable to that provided by competitor nations;
- sustain a culture which demands disciplined thinking, encourages curiosity, challenges existing ideas and generates new ones;
- be part of the conscience of a democratic society, founded on respect for the rights of the individual and the responsibilities of the individual to society as a whole;
- be explicit and clear in how it goes about its business, be accountable to students and to society, and seek continuously to improve its own performance.

To achieve this, higher education will depend on:

- professional, committed members of staff who are appropriately trained, respected and rewarded;
- a diverse range of autonomous, well-managed institutions with commitment to excellence in the achievement of their distinctive missions.

Dearing can be seen as a fuller working out of the ethos of a university set out by Robbins and the need to increase opportunity set in the context of present needs. It also recognised the various roles of different parts of the higher education system and an emphasis on life-long learning. Over the preceding 20 years the number of students in higher education had doubled while public funding had increased in real terms by 45 per cent and the unit of funding per student fallen by 40 per cent. Public spending on universities as a percentage of GDP had remained constant. Clearly this could not continue if the ambitions for higher education were to be met and so the question of how to pay became a major policy issue and the committee recommended that government consider the possibility of some student contribution to costs. It recommended a fee of

£1000 to be paid by means of a graduate tax. The Report ran to 2000 pages with 95 important recommendations, but the proposal for fees was a watershed. Nevertheless, the guiding principles were little different from those of the Robbins Report.

By the time the Dearing Committee reported (1997) Labour was in power. It had made an election promise to stick with Tory spending plans for two years, but faced with the need to restore some of the cuts in the 1980s and the prospect of increasing participation it introduced a 'top-up fee' of £1000, with some alleviation for students from low income families, while maintaining the level of university grants. This was an upfront payment – the recommendation for a graduate tax was rejected – and loans were not available. The relief for low income families meant that around one third of students did not pay. Maintenance grants were scrapped and replaced by loans to be repaid on an income contingent basis. In 2003 policy reverted to one closer to the Dearing recommendation. Fees were increased to £3000 but as an income-contingent loan and maintenance grants were reintroduced. The Higher Education Act 2004 which introduced this policy also provided for an Office for Fair Access (OFFA) and, for student complaints, an Office of the Independent Adjudicator (OIA). The first of these was to monitor universities' policies for providing access to disadvantaged students. A university which wished to charge above the existing level (by that time £1125) up to the £3000 maximum was required to have a plan for a bursary scheme to subsidise qualifying students up to the fee set by their university and this had to be approved by OFFA. Almost all universities decided to charge the maximum £3000. The OIA replaced the antiquated 'visitorial' system (which did not in any case apply to the former polytechnics) to adjudicate on student complaints which remained unresolved by the host university. Each of these bodies were set up to deal with potential problems seen by opponents to the proposed fees policy – the first to deal with access, the second to deal with the likelihood of an increase in complaints from students having to pay significant fees. The 2004 Act also set up the Arts and Humanities Research Council, replacing the Arts and Humanities Research Board. There was considerable opposition to the Act from all sides and in its 2005 election manifesto the Conservative Party pledged to abolish fees.

In 2010, the Labour government commissioned the Browne Report which shifted the debate from one of how to increase participation to how to improve quality by the introduction of a market and competition. It is interesting to see how the Browne Report moved the issue of fees on from the Dearing Report. Dearing introduced tuition fees to be paid by students. This was mainly as a consequence of the straits to which universities had been reduced by a number of inconsistent policies, first by constraint on numbers and then expansion without an increase in unit resource so that the only way for a university to maintain its teaching income was to take more students at a lower unit of resource. As noted above, Dearing proposed a fee of £1000 per year of study repayable by a graduate tax. Fees were seen as a financial necessity, rather than as part of a market that would improve quality through competition.

The Browne Report (2010) ran to 64 pages. It proposed replacing the teaching grant (with a few exceptions) by a fee of £6000 per year of study repayable with interest through the tax system on an income-contingent basis with universities able to charge more (up to a maximum of £9000) on condition that a proportion of this extra fee be paid to the public purse in recognition of the extra liability this imposed (by potential non-payment of loans in full). The interest rate would be the same as that the government has to pay for its own loans. Government would set a cap on overall student numbers. The four regulatory bodies would be replaced by one – a Higher Education Council – which would allocate special funds for high cost or priority courses.

Among the benefits the Report promised were more competition, emphasis on quality (deriving from competition), less government regulation, more trust in the decisions of students and universities. In recognition that competition might endanger standards it was recommended that the Higher Education Council would enforce 'standards of quality'. It is unclear whether this meant standards of service to students or academic standards of the degrees awarded. It is notable that the principles identified as 'intrinsic to the Higher Education System' are 'participation (meeting qualified demand), quality (flowing from competition based on price and teaching quality within a framework of minimum standards) and sustainability (via increased private investment and targeted public investment)'.

Browne contrasts significantly to Robbins or Dearing, perhaps not unrelated to the fact that his report was commissioned by the Department for Business, Innovation and Skills, which had taken over responsibility for universities.

In summary, the arguments for change were:

- The ambition to increase the number of undergraduates would lead to increased costs and a student contribution would go some way to meeting this.
- The view that since graduates on average earn more by virtue of their education they should contribute to the cost.
- Transferring costs to students would create a competitive market and improve quality and efficiency.

The Browne Report was accepted by government but its recommendations were significantly modified in practice. We will argue in this book that in fact the modifications were much more profound in impact than the government recognised. Government set an upper limit on fees at £9000 without the restraint imposed by Browne's recommended clawback from fees above £6000. The fees were repayable as an income-contingent loan by a 9 per cent surcharge on income tax on earnings above £21,000 and attracting an interest rate up to RPI plus 3 per cent, contrary to the Browne recommendation that it should be set at no more than the rate the government itself pays. Universities would be allowed to charge above £6000 only if they had plans to improve access to disadvantaged groups approved by OFFA. The clawback of a percentage of fee above £6000 recommended by Browne was not adopted. Fees would replace grants in all subjects except those with high teaching costs. Subsequently, in 2015, government announced the rejection of Browne's recommendation for a limit on overall student numbers and the cap was removed.

Other recommendations were incorporated in the 2017 Higher Education and Research Act. This Act established a new regulatory system recognising the shift away from grant funding (and therefore a reduced role for HEFCE) towards funding through fees paid by students. The new system was focused on the idea that there was a need for better information on which student choice can be made, of which the Teaching Excellence Framework (TEF) is an example.

The new Office for Students (OfS) will incorporate the roles of HEFCE and OFFA. The Quality and Assurance Agency (QAA) will remain independent (but inform the work of the OfS) as will the OIA, HESA (Higher Education and Statistics Agency) and UCAS (the University and College Admissions Service). The role of the OIA would expand to cover all institutions recognised by OfS. The OfS will have powers to recognise and regulate new providers, the explicit intention being to make it easier for new private providers to enter the system and for their students to be eligible for government loans. The Student Loans Company will continue as present. A first round of TEF assessments has taken place, effectively an attempt to rank universities by the quality of their teaching, a ranking which is intended to be used to introduce more effective competition and better inform student choice. The Act also brought together existing Research Councils under the umbrella of 'UK Research and Innovation' with the intention of facilitating national research priorities and encouraging interdisciplinary research.

Particularly as fees and living expenses (such as accommodation costs) have risen to high levels, and maintenance grants have largely disappeared, the structure of the student loan system has become fundamental to both universities and their students. Large loans for higher education are unlikely to be available from the private sector. Like mortgages, these loans are long-term in nature which is unattractive to banks. Unlike mortgages, there is no good security in the form of real estate. Lenders would need to validate degrees and ensure that the student was studying hard to have a realistic chance of repayment. While this provides a rationale for government provision of student loans, there remains an irony that those espousing greater marketisation simultaneously require that it be supported by the government.

Given the fundamental role for student loans, it may be helpful to summarise the recent history of loans to put the current situation in context.[3]

- Before 1998 student loans were available for living costs at an interest rate of RPI minus 1.6 per cent, repayable above an income threshold of £29,126.
- From 1998 to 2006 there was an upfront fee of £1000 together with loans for maintenance with no interest, paid by a 9 per cent tax surcharge on incomes above £21,000.
- From 2006 to 2012 the £1000 cap was raised to £3000 (increased to £3225 in 2009). Interest was charged at RPI or 1 per cent above Bank Rate, whichever was the lower. Repayment started at a salary of £15,000 (increasing to £17,495 by 2012). Means-tested grants were re-introduced, supplemented by income-contingent loans with interest at RPI +1 per cent.
- From 2012 the fee cap was raised to £9,000, effectively replacing the teaching grant except for high cost subjects. Interest was at RPI + 3 per cent while studying, RPI + 0-3 per cent on a sliding scale after graduation. Repayment was by a 9 per cent tax surcharge on incomes above £21,000. Maintenance grants were scrapped and replaced with additional loans.
- Access to student loans opened to students of 'alternative providers' since 2012 rose from 7000 students to 53,000 resulting in £1.271 billion in loans to such students. The extent to which these loans are unpaid amounts to a public subsidy to these providers. Some providers identified as 'rogue suppliers' with £3.84 million being paid to ineligible students.[4]

Without commenting for the moment on current policy, it may be observed that with such frequent changes successive generations of students have been treated differently and the costs have been a lottery depending on one's age. It might be noted that all political parties have recognised the political difficulties of the fees policies. However, any substantial lowering or elimination of fees for the future (as proposed by Labour) raises further intergenerational equity issues, particularly on the question of writing off existing debt. The current policy therefore has already developed considerable momentum.

In parallel to these changes the system for ensuring standards and teaching quality has been modified. This function was first taken on by the Higher Education Quality Council in 1992 under the Committee of Vice-Chancellors and Principals (CVCP). It undertook subject reviews (grading departments) and Academic Audit (inspecting institutional systems). In 1997, these two functions were brought together as the QAA under the auspices of HEFCE with the remit to monitor standards and the quality of teaching and to promote systematic improvement. After concerns were raised that the QAA had not been effective in maintaining standards a parliamentary enquiry in 2008 confirmed this view. Subsequently contributing to these concerns was the fact that under the coalition government the number of private providers increased considerably raising concerns about standards in general and 'phoney' colleges enrolling unqualified overseas students. QAA was asked to pay more attention to this part of the system under the auspices of the UK Border Control Agency and subsequently UK Visas and Immigration. As a result, it was agreed that QAA would give established universities a 'lighter touch'.

Although we have tried to set a historical policy context in this chapter, the main purpose of this book is an attempt to analyse the effects of the move to the current fee and oversight regime and the aim of the Browne Report to introduce a market and competition into higher education. We take as a good yardstick the principles and objectives laid down in the Dearing Report and how the new landscape serves those ambitions from the point of view of public finances, the student experience, academic standards, the internal management of universities, and the place of universities in the higher education system.

We think that the tradition in Robbins and Dearing was a valuable one, and that the nature of universities in England was shifted profoundly by the introduction of the market and the high fee regime. Each of the major political parties has had a no fees pledge in its manifesto in a recent election, yet each has been involved in increasing fees to more and more substantial levels. Further, each of the constituent countries in the UK has set up its own system. Wales initially subsidised fees, but has subsequently withdrawn that support, although is now reviewing its policy, while Northern Ireland continues to set fees for local students at roughly half the English level. The Student Awards Agency for Scotland continues to pay the low (£1820) fees set for eligible Scottish students attending Scottish universities, so Scotland is effectively offering free tuition. In addition, the real interest rate on student loans is 0 per cent in Scotland and not the significantly above-market rate currently offered in England. In the Short Note, we consider the case for free tuition in general and the Scottish system in particular.

A Short Note On: The Case for Free Tuition and the Scottish Approach

Generally, throughout this book we are considering the government's overall approach to university funding on its own terms. In particular, we have constrained ourselves not to propose any new funding for the sector in light of the overall fiscal austerity, and have also accepted that funding should largely follow students in terms of the fees that they pay. We do want to pause for a moment, however, and consider the case for the alternative system – adopted in Scotland – of having zero fees paid by students. There are numerous examples of zero fee publicly-provided services in the UK. In London, individuals over 66 are eligible for a valuable Freedom Pass entitling them to zero fees across all of London Transport. The NHS is free at the point of service. Most major museums have become free to enter since 2001. The individual gains private benefits from each of these services on offer, in the same way as university students gain private benefits, but the government has nonetheless decided not to charge. It is interesting to note the amount that accumulates in the 'contributions' boxes in museums and galleries. This demonstrates an appreciation of the free admissions policy and of the value of the experience. This may provide lessons for the potential of lifetime voluntary donations from alumni in appreciation of their undergraduate experience – and encourage universities to recognise this.

Arguments can be made in each of these cases that there would be some gain in economic efficiency if fees were levied. The underground and buses are crowded at peak hours, so perhaps those over 66 could pay a reduced charge rather than have free travel. A modest charge for GP appointments might lead to fewer 'wasted' appointments, often where elderly patients are simply seeking social interaction. The economic efficiency arguments are however often over-stated. For example, having a patient avoid the GP due to a charge and spreading a contagious disease would be a false economy. Similarly, delayed treatment is both more expensive and less effective. Nonetheless, one can argue that a modest fee can be more efficient in all these cases.

There are three reasons why the government might prefer to set zero fees rather than the modest fee that a calculus of marginal costs and benefits might dictate. One is that 'the game is not worth the candle'. Is it really worth setting up an expensive IT system to collect a few pounds from each individual GP appointment? A second is that there tends to be drift. A zero fee tends to remain a zero fee, but a £1 fee quickly mutates into a £2 fee and so on, as an easy source of additional revenue. We have seen this in university fees, where £1000 became £3000 and then suddenly jumped to £9000.

The third reason, however, is, we think, the most important. Setting a zero fee is a clear statement of the values of our society. Nowhere is this clearer than in the NHS, which we want to be a common experience for all segments of society. We want to separate out cost from medical treatment, in the same way that – in countries without an NHS – a family might ensure that a less well-off member received necessary medical treatment without any concern for the cost. The NHS, free at the point of service, reflects who we are as a nation and it is not surprising that it formed part of the Olympics opening ceremony in London, even if it bemused spectators from other countries.

With university fees, there are good reasons why they should be heavily subsidised. It is generally accepted that high quality education is a public good as well as a private one. The public good element should be met from general taxation on both economic efficiency and fairness grounds. There are significant externalities to having a highly-educated workforce. Further, the personal enrichment gained in a high-quality university experience is also a contribution to the public good in the sense that it contributes to a more settled society and a public better equipped to contribute to a healthy democracy. Degree educated individuals may take jobs that while not highly paid serve the community in worthwhile ways such as teaching and nursing, or in the arts. Even if all the gains from a university education were private, economic efficiency requires a significant subsidy. The private financial gain from a university education is already taxed and high earners pay a high marginal tax rate through the progressive income tax system as well as more VAT through higher spending. Simple algebra shows that the rate of subsidy should be at least the marginal rate of tax and national insurance, for higher earnings well in excess of 50 per cent.

We feel that there is a strong argument, as in Scotland, to go the rest of the way and fully subsidise fees. This is in part to shift attention away from the earnings effects of a university education – which are distorting in terms of the student's choice of university and course – and to emphasise the role of university as a place for academic and creative challenges and debate. Government policy has gone in the opposite direction. For example, recent proposals from the OfS are to grade universities on the salaries achieved by their graduates. We view this as a stunning misunderstanding of the purposes of a university and reveals the philosophy of the architects of the scheme. In the same way, students who take A levels are likely to earn more than those who do not, even without going to university, but nobody argues that they should pay to go into sixth form. There is an argument in support of fees for very specific courses for professional qualification, such as accountancy, where standards and certification rest with the professional body. Otherwise, the case made by some that students should pay for state provided education derives more from a particular philosophy than on economic efficiency. That philosophy is permeating into the life of universities to the detriment of those qualities that have in the past contributed to the high regard in which they have been held. That zero fees would be affordable is seen by contrasting German expenditure on Higher Education (3 per cent) with our own (1.7 per cent).

Even with zero fees, students attending university while not living at home will have large rental and maintenance costs. For reasons of widening participation, maintenance grants have in the past (but not now) been available to students from lower income households, but other students have incurred the full cost of maintenance. This can be justified on the basis that the student would need to eat and have somewhere to live, even if they were not attending university. Fees, in contrast, are only incurred as a result of attending university.

In the Scottish system, funded student places remain capped at each university and the bulk of funding comes through a block teaching grant of about £6000 per student. Fees are currently set at £1820, but a Scottish student can normally have these paid by the Student Awards Agency for Scotland. Note that, since some block grant remains in place in England, in addition to current fees of £9250, the per student funding in Scotland is in total substantially below the per student funding in England. This suggests that a reduction in fees in England to £7500 – with savings to both students and taxpayers – would not be unduly onerous on the university sector. Even better – in our view – those funds could come back to the sector in return for better performance in the quality of education and in widening participation.

Either because of this funding differential, or because of the different systems – primarily block grant in Scotland versus fee-funded in England – there is some evidence that Scottish universities have fallen behind in league tables. See Table 2.1 for a comparison of the 2019 to the 2011 Guardian league table standings for the top Scottish universities.

Table 2.1: League table standings of Scottish universities

	2011	2019
St Andrews	3	3
Edinburgh	15	28
Dundee	22	29
Glasgow	23	24
Strathclyde	25	53
Robert Gordon	27	78
Stirling	27	40
Heriot-Watt	32	66
Aberdeen	33	51

It is not possible, based on the information available, to try to determine whether the slippage in Scotland relative to England is due to the lesser funding levels per student, or due to the difference in the system. Further, as we shall argue later in the book, these league tables are predominantly based upon National Student Survey scores, and are therefore measuring satisfaction rather than the quality of education. In contrast to the NSS (National Student Survey), which we consider pointless, we do value the results in the Research Excellence Framework (REF), and will await with interest the 2021 REF to see if in fact Scottish universities have slipped relative to English ones in the international quality of their research.

3

Markets Without Competition

Economics today has become a matter of predetermined slogans such as 'more markets' or – on the alternative political side – 'more regulation'. In practice, any efficient system has to be a combination of competition and regulation, even if the taxpayer is not – as is the case with universities – picking up the bulk of the bills. However, when the sector is heavily subsidised, the distortions of either unfettered markets or micromanaged regulation can become amplified. There is 'rent seeking' as participants try to divert the subsidies to their own interests. This can be facilitated by 'regulatory capture' where the institutions being regulated become too close to the regulators and have undue influence on the decisions made.

The emphasis should be on designing an intelligent and effective mechanism for achieving clear desired ends. There cannot be markets for their own sake – irrespective of the efficiency of the outcomes – or similarly regulation to make up for poor design of the allocation mechanism. As is often the case, 'the best is the enemy of the good'. No market will be so perfect as to achieve ideal outcomes, and all regulation is costly. We will discuss in Chapter Four how the allocation of decision-making power to different stakeholders can help bridge the gap between what the regulated market can do on its own, and what we are trying to achieve on behalf of the students and taxpayers. But for now, we are just trying to get 'in the ballpark' of a sensible system.

What we are trying to achieve, based upon the Robbins, Dearing and Browne reports described in the previous chapter are:

- a high quality of education
- value for money
- widening participation

We will discuss in this chapter how the system proposed in the Browne Report could have worked reasonably well, but that the switch to higher fees than proposed (£9000 rather than £6000) and uncapped student numbers led to disastrous results in terms of the nature of competition. Rather than a competition over education quality directed at the best students potentially available to the university, competition became that of the 'lowest common denominator'. It was aimed at the weaker students and took the form − disproportionately − of grade inflation.

The problems

Once universities were uncapped in admissions, the elite and Russell Group universities hugely expanded their intakes at the expense of the other pre-1992 and the post-1992 institutions (see Figure 3.1).

Figure 3.1: First year students

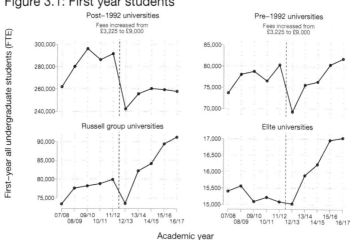

Note: The Open University is excluded in this figure as part of the pre-1992 universities. Including the OU would increase the drop in student numbers in 2012/13 and reduce the increase in the following years.

Source: HESA Student Record 2007/08–2016/17

The question for the other universities was in how to compete against these strongest players. We will later argue that these other institutions need to compete by finding their own Unique Selling Proposition. Further, while the non-Russell pre-1992 universities are generally able to find a 'boutique' market position with fewer students but maintaining quality comparable to the Russell Group, the task facing most of the post-1992 institutions is different. They also should go back to their heritage and define features that make them unique, but it may be the case that – in the hierarchical world of higher education – they need to set lower fees to attract well-prepared students. We will come back to this when we discuss widening participation in Chapter Six and our policy proposals in Chapter Seven.

In practice, 'competition' took the form of grade inflation. The average 'tariff' of A-level results for students in each of the university types remained fairly static since the introduction of high fees, in part because previous grade inflation in A-levels had come under control. There was a modest falling-off in entry scores, with the exception of the post-1992 universities (where entry numbers have declined) (see Figure 3.2).

Despite the students remaining of roughly the same capability on average, at least as measured by A level points at the point of entry, the class of degrees awarded exploded (see Figure 3.3). The proportion of upper second degrees remained roughly constant over time, while third-class degrees showed a modest tailing-off. However, first-class degrees went up sharply – from about 10 per cent to 20 per cent for the system as a whole – while the proportion of lower seconds fell sharply – from 35 per cent to 20 per cent.

Ironically, this grade inflation has the effect of further boosting the Russell Group universities, particularly at the expense of the non-Russell pre-1992 universities. Previously, a student might be advised to go to a non-Russell university because the course matched the student's interests and abilities, the geographical location fitted the student's preferences, smaller size and campus environments enabled easier socialising with students outside one's own department and a good student would get additional attention that they might not get at the very top universities. The student would be able to signal by the classification of degree – a first or a strong upper second – that they had put in the effort,

Figure 3.2: Average entry tariff

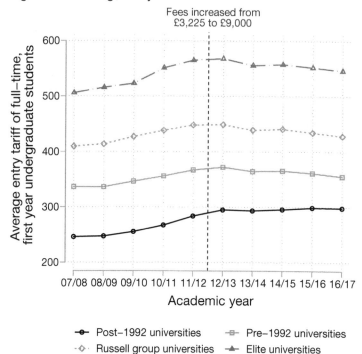

Source: HESA Student Record 2007/08–2016/17

Figure 3.3: Awarded degree classifications

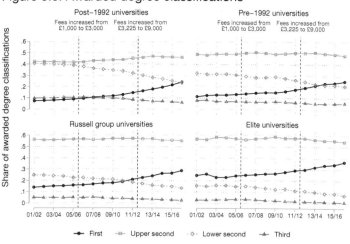

Source: HESA Student Record 2001/02–2016/17

and had the ability to succeed, especially given the UK tradition of an understanding across the sector of what constitutes a 'good' degree. But if the strong majority of students at the non-Russell universities are getting 'good degrees', upper seconds and firsts, that signalling effect is gone. The only way to signal ability is by going to a Russell Group university.

The bottom line is that, by competing on grade inflation rather than the quality of education, the non-Russell pre-1992 universities are worsening their competitive position over time, in a downward spiral. We now turn to why the structure set up by the government encouraged this self-destructive market without competition.

The hierarchy of universities

The nature of universities is that they are hierarchical. Cambridge, Oxford and Imperial College represent elite universities, internationally recognised as among the top ten universities in the world. The LSE and UCL are not far behind and we have included them in our category of elite university when we present our numerical analyses. The hierarchy continues through the Russell Group, which has – particularly after the introduction of £9000 fees – effectively established itself as being 'the leading, world-class universities' in the UK. Traditionally following this are the remaining pre-1992 universities and finally the post-1992 universities. The recent paper by Andrew Jenkins and Alison Wolf[1] shows that this hierarchy continues to have a very strong impact on the income per student of a university. This is despite the case that, in some league tables, some of the other pre-1992 universities dominate Russell Group universities, and that some of the post-1992 universities come out ahead of some of the more established pre-1992 universities.

The idea of the fees-driven market was that universities would compete over the quality of education and value for money. We argue throughout this book that positive competition was entirely feasible – every English university has distinctive strengths that could be the foundation for a first-rate learning environment. Indeed, departments and universities vigorously competed on research and teaching before the introduction of the market. We want to get a grasp on why the new system actually led to a diminution of real (education quality based) competition, and compare the outcomes to other possible systems.

The methodology used in Economics is not well understood in public discourse, perhaps because the professional journals are predominantly mathematical and statistical in nature. They are consequently virtually impossible for non-economists to read. This is not the place to debate in depth the role of mathematics in Economics which we see as being about clarity in exposition and economy in presentation. Simply put, it is a lot shorter and more precise to write an equation rather than to express the same thoughts verbally. Leaving aside the mathematical expression of economic analysis, what is fundamental is that economists work with 'models'. A model is a very simplified example that is designed to bring out clearly how something works. A good model is one that is simple but captures the most salient features of the mechanism being explored. Because of the extent of judgement involved in constructing a model, it can never be a definitive answer but can only be a guide to how to think about a problem and how to avoid serious policy mistakes. In the case of university funding mechanisms, we can see what could have gone wrong, provide empirical evidence as to whether or not that is what has happened and suggest possible better approaches.

We now set up a model to try to get a clear vision on why competition might be extinguished rather than enhanced by the fees-driven market system. We consider the very real issue of a 'regular' university in the same ecosystem as an elite Russell Group university. There is a pool of potential students. Some of these students are 'first-class' and some are 'second-class' measured by the likelihood of the classification of degree they would get at a university following traditional standards of assessment. This sort of ability and effort applied is typically measured at entry by A-level grades. In a later chapter on widening participation, we discuss the problems with this basis for admissions, but for now we recognise that that is the system as it historically and currently operates.

Students of different abilities and effort may want different things from a university. Our discussion in this chapter is based upon the idea that 'first-class' students are primarily focused on the academic side of the university, although they will also typically want good sporting facilities and cheap beer in the student union. Although the model we present here recognises the very hierarchical nature of universities, we think it a mistake pedagogically to assume that 'second-class' students are only concerned with 'bread and circuses' and don't also want a challenging academic environment and often additional support to make up for shortcomings in their past preparation.

The student

The student gains value from going to university. This may be due to enhanced 'employability', with the student gaining a higher lifetime income or achieving a career they seek not solely dictated by income. Alternatively, the value of going to university may arise from lifelong friendships and from the advantage of being exposed to intellectual debate and diverse cultural influences, and have little to do with simple 'employability' at all. In choosing whether or not to go to university, or which university or course to undertake, the student won't know the future precisely, but can estimate the potential value.

Economic models are normally written with symbols, so that we can write out a general framework. Here, for ease of understanding, we use a symbol but also provide a numerical example. The basic return to going to any university might be written as the symbol J; for a numerical example, we might view this as in the range of £60,000. That is, it pretty much just about pays for a student to incur the current level of fees and maintenance costs when they go to a university away from home.

Students gain a further value from being awarded a 'first-class degree'. They are more employable provided that potential employers believe that a first-class degree is a meaningful signal and hasn't been eroded by grade inflation. For the moment, we will assume that universities have maintained standards and accurately label a student of first-class ability and effort with a first-class degree, and students of second-class ability and effort with a second-class degree. We can write the symbol K as the value of gaining a first-class degree; for a numerical example, we might view this as in the range of £20,000.

Finally, there is value gained from going to an elite university. Whether or not it is fair, a student with an Oxbridge degree is in general more employable in a graduate level job than one from a less prestigious university. Some students in addition particularly value the historical and other aspects of Oxbridge, or Imperial College, or the LSE or UCL. At these universities, eminent visiting scholars, politicians and authors regularly visit and give talks. There are vibrant student societies. In contrast to the previous two values – the basic return to going to university and the value of a first-class degree – the gain to going to an elite university depends upon individual students' preferences. Some students, on a visit to Cambridge, value the old buildings and College system – where they mingle fully with students on a range of degree subjects – very highly. Others (and this is associated with serious widening participation issues) feel uncomfortable and that they wouldn't belong. The same factors hold, albeit to a lesser extent, for a comparison between a Russell Group university and another extremely solid academic institution that nonetheless lacks the Russell Group cachet.

Using symbols, we can write V as the value gained by a student going to an elite university who highly values that experience, and v as the smaller value gained by a student going to an elite university who is less focused upon institutional prestige. For a numerical example, a student really focused on an elite university (think for example of Alan Bennett's play *The History Boys*) might gain £40,000 and a student less intent on going there might gain £10,000. This second group of students will be very important in our discussion since the regular university might try to attract some of these students away from the elite university by offering a programme that is better directed towards their particular interests, or that provides a higher standard of teaching.

Putting all this together, we can summarise the values to students in Table 3.1.

Table 3.1: Values to the student from attending university

	Elite university	Regular university
First-class student – strongly prefers elite university	J + K + V £120,000	J + K £80,000
First-class student – weakly prefers elite university	J + K + v £90,000	J + K £80,000
Second-class student – strongly prefers elite university	J + V £100,000	J £60,000
Second-class student – weakly prefers elite university	J + v £70,000	J £60,000

The first-class student who really values being at an elite university, who gains a place there, is the biggest beneficiary from the system. The second-class student, under our assumptions to this point, who goes to the regular university, is the marginal student in the sense of comparing the value gained from attendance to the costs of attendance and possibly deciding not to go to university at all.

The university

Universities have an average cost of educating students. We go along with Browne, and our own simple arithmetic calculations, and view £6000 as the basic per student cost. Each university also has a capacity constraint, at least in the short run. Finally, we recognise that academics prefer to recruit and teach the most capable students. This might be the case since it is easier or more rewarding to teach a good student, or because having good students enhances the status of the university.

Browne and the government's response to Browne was based upon the idea that a market type system would encourage universities to compete for students by enhancing the quality of education, or by increasing 'value for money' by increased efficiency that could lead to price competition. Few participants in the sector, however, were surprised that nearly all universities set the maximum £9000 fee for their courses. Setting a lower fee would be a signal that the programme wasn't up to the general standard. We had already seen that when £3000 maximum fees were set all universities set fees at the maximum allowed. Further, all universities set uncontrolled overseas student fees at high levels, typically well in excess of £9000.

In the absence of price competition, universities could still vigorously compete for students. They did so before the high-fee, uncapped student-numbers system was put in place. A regular university would try to establish programmes such that good students would want to attend. Top students might value small classes and tutorials, and the chance to have one-to-one discussions with the most distinguished professors at the institution. A university could offer programmes in specialist subjects, or concentrate its strengths in some academic areas, to attract these first-class students. In contrast, second-class students might be more concerned with the vocational elements of the programme in the hope that this will open up more job prospects. Some expenditures, such as new sporting facilities, could be aimed at both types of potential students. More negatively, grade inflation can occur – this benefits the weaker students at the expense of the better students who would have earned a top degree in any case. We will argue that the uncapped numbers and high fees adopted encouraged grade inflation competition rather than competition by offering better academic programmes and more intensive teaching from leading research academics.

Grade inflation

Grade inflation is not a 'victimless crime'. As seen in the charts earlier in the chapter, the percentage of first-class degrees has gone up sharply, and that of third-class degrees has gone down. Effectively, a student who would previously have got an upper second will now have an enhanced probability of getting a first, and so on. Grade inflation matters since a given degree class becomes no longer a clear signal of the student's effort and ability, and consequent achievement in their chosen subject. In the absence of grade inflation, in our simple model above, a first-class student gets a first-class degree and an employer can confidently expect the graduate to perform at that level. With grade inflation, however, some second-class students will also get first-class degrees and the employer will no longer have a clear signal that the new employee is of top ability and effort.

We will consider why universities have competed by grade inflation rather than by improving their academic programmes or lowering their fees. There are, however, important implications. Grade inflation arises when the university is seeking to make its offer more attractive to the weaker, not the stronger students. The effective response of the top students is to try more desperately to gain admittance to the top universities, letting the university name be the signal of the student's accomplishments. If a non-Russell university offers the otherwise perfect programme for the student, the first-class student is nonetheless well-advised to find a Russell university with a less appropriate programme. The hierarchy of universities becomes ever more established.

The pre-Browne system

Before the increase in fees, each university had an agreed headcount with HEFCE and received income both from the fixed fees (£3000) and the block grant (averaging about £3000 per student). Browne, in his report, thought that fees of £6000 (in the absence of the block grant except for some particularly high cost subjects) would just about match existing funding and involve just a small amount of tightening for universities. It should be noted that the agreed headcount for each university had evolved over time as one that was comfortable for the university and encouraged long-term planning and sensible investment. Universities were neither going bankrupt nor were they awash in cash, since the £6000 just about covered the costs of education.

We consider the effects of this traditional system. For simplicity, we add a further assumption, that HEFCE set the same headcount for each of our two universities. The first issue concerns the types of students who go to university. If the headcount is very low, then both universities can adopt very selective admissions policies and only admit first-class students. At the £3000 fee level, there would be no problem recruiting these students, who would gain – even at the regular university – a value well in excess of their fees. This would be a very elite university system where only a modest percentage of the population would attend. The Robbins Report (1963) made clear that the future needs of the country required a more inclusive and expanded university system.

In practice, therefore, with the expansion in higher education after the Robbins Report, HEFCE set headcounts such that not only the top students would go to university. At the relatively low fees of £3000, universities did not have undue difficulty in filling this higher number of places. The only real issue was how students were allocated across the universities. If the headcount allocated to the elite university was greater than the number of top students in the system, the elite university would offer places to all the first-class students. In the absence of some special effort by the regular but not elite university, these first-class students would choose to go to the elite university and gain the extra value from doing so. If the headcount allocated to the elite university fell short of the number of top students, then some of the first-class students would of necessity go to the regular university, having failed to gain places at the elite university.

Even if there were places for all the top students at the elite university, the regular university might compete for them. Some students are not as wedded to going to the elite university as are others. By offering students better teaching or a better environment, or academic scholarships, the regular university can attract some students away from the elite university. The elite university might accept the loss of these students provided that they were relatively low in number. While we have modelled the situation where a regular university is competing with an elite one, the same sort of quality of education competition for top students could occur between two regular universities or between two elite universities.

Under the old system, a student in the Arts might well choose to go to Goldsmiths over UCL. An economics student might prefer Warwick to Cambridge. Each university could find its niche, and attract good students in limited numbers. Put in a less positive way, the LSE might use a lot of graduate student teaching of undergraduates, knowing that most students will nonetheless want to go there for the prestige. The LSE would accept that a modest number of top students might prefer to go elsewhere where greater effort is put into teaching the best students. This is very much institutionalised in the United States where state universities often offer 'Honours' programmes to the best students, with small classes and individualised attention. 'Liberal arts' colleges compete for the best students by offering a more personalised approach than do the Ivy League universities, which are often focused upon PhD students.

For these reasons, it was simply not the case that there was no competition between universities pre-Browne. At relatively low fees, and with capped student numbers, universities did not have to compete for student 'bodies', but instead would compete for the quality of their student intake. Academics highly value the prestige of their department and their university. They go to great efforts not just to progress their own research through publications and grants, but to recruit other top academics to enhance the reputation of the subject group and the university. They seek to attract top PhD students. Under the traditional system, academics would engage in open days to recruit good undergraduates, with some departments still having individual interviews of prospective students which served not just as a selection mechanism but an advertisement that they cared while at the same time showing that an offer of a place was an achievement and, in a sense, a sort of informal contract – 'we believe you have what it takes and will help you achieve'.

Grade inflation would have had a negative impact in this competition for top students. Grade inflation benefits the weaker students at the expense of better students. It would be particularly important for the first-class student, choosing to go to a less prestigious university because the course or environment was better for them, to know that the first-class degree eventually obtained was recognised externally as being equivalent to that from Imperial College or the LSE. If anything, these other universities needed to be even more precious than the elite universities in preserving the value of their first-class degrees.

The Browne proposal of capped student numbers

Browne essentially proposed fixing the maximum total number of students in the sector, but not at particular universities. This would be done in practice by each year setting a minimum UCAS points standard for qualifying for a loan. Universities could compete for these students. Browne also proposed that universities could charge higher fees than £6000, but these would be subject to high and eventually punitive 'taxation' in terms of a levy on the additional fee income. It seems unlikely to us that a university would take up this possibility, given that the levy starts at 40 per cent (at fees of £7000, payable on the £1000 extra fee level) and rises to 75 per cent (at fees of £12,000). Browne, however, argues that the levy essentially recovers the subsidy to student loans, from the non-repayment percentage, on the additional fees. As noted, we will, in the following, assume a non-payment rate of 50 per cent on fees due to loan write-off, consistent with many estimates and expectations and in the 40 –75 per cent range of the levy levels proposed by Browne on higher fees. Nonetheless, we will continue the discussion on the basis that each university avoids the levy by setting fees of £6000.

We begin by assuming that the total number of students is capped at a level that is the same as under the individual headcounts in the traditional system before Browne (remember we are working on a simplified model with just two universities). Browne actually proposed a 10 per cent increase in student numbers. We should pause a moment and consider whether or not there is likely to be an increased or even maintained demand for places, given that fees have doubled under the Browne proposals from the earlier £3000 to £6000. If each student anticipates a write-off of 50 per cent on the loan repayments under the contingent-repayment loan scheme (unable to make assumptions about their own individual future earnings), then – if there is no interest payment on loans – the calculation on whether or not to go to university is unchanged since the average payment is still £3000. However, Browne did propose that interest be charged for successful graduates (at the government 's own rate of borrowing), so under the scheme there is potentially a shortfall in demand for places.

We will discuss the loan scheme in more detail in Chapter Six. In fact, we will argue that the contingent loan scheme rewards weak programmes and failure, and therefore that a good student on a well-chosen programme receives very little or no subsidy at all. The rise in fees, even to the proposed £6000, much less the actual £9000 might well deter some potential highly qualified students. As we discuss in Chapter Six, the high interest rates on the loan scheme mean that it is actually regressive in the sense that high-earning graduates will pay back less than some middle-income graduates over their careers. The reason is that high earners pay off their debt early with a lower total cost. If this becomes more widely understood it will present a further deterrent. For now, however, we assume – as the data indicates to date – that there are ample students seeking places across the system as a whole, if not necessarily at each individual university.

Under the Browne scheme, the elite university (and the regular university) are not individually capped, but can seek to 'poach' student numbers from the other university. In practice, the incentives to recruit additional students seem at first sight to be somewhat limited, since the £6000 fee per student just roughly covers the cost of education. However, some of that cost is fixed overheads, which are incurred by the university whether or not a marginal number of extra students are recruited. The marginal cost incurred by the university from educating one more student will be considerably less than £6000, giving an incentive to expand. This potential for 'poaching' is the basis of the competition envisaged by Browne.

We have discussed how academics prefer to recruit the best students, and will put in considerable effort to do so. If the elite university decides to expand from the pre-Browne HEFCE headcount up to its capacity, it will seek to admit the best students available to it, and then fill any remaining places with weaker students. The elite university will seek to admit more first-class students than before, and is less likely than before to leave any for the regular university. But not only will the regular university then have fewer top students than before, it will have fewer students in total due to the overall headcount imposed by the Browne system.

It may be helpful to have an example with specific student numbers in mind. Let's suppose that each university previously had a headcount of 1000 so that the total headcount over the two universities under Browne is set at 2000 students. Suppose that the capacity of the elite university is 1500 and there are only 1000 first class students in the population going to university. Further, 80 per cent of students have a high preference for going to the elite university, and 20 per cent have the lower preference for going to the elite university. Then the default situation, where the elite university chooses its admissions and the regular university does not take steps to respond with vigorous competition is shown in Table 3.2.

Table 3.2: Example of numbers of students of each type

	Elite university	Regular university
First-class student – strongly prefers elite university	800	0
First-class student – weakly prefers elite university	200	0
Second-class student – strongly prefers elite university	400	400
Second-class student – weakly prefers elite university	100	100

The elite university first admits all the first-class students. Under the pre-Browne HEFCE cap, the elite university would have been capped at 1000 students and stopped there. With the Browne sector (but not individual university) cap, the elite university fills its remaining places up to capacity (assumed to be 1500) with 500 second-class students. In our example, 500 student places are left over for the regular university. Admissions at the regular university have fallen by half compared to the pre-Browne regime where HEFCE allocated fixed numbers of students to each university.

The regular university considers how to compete. It can tailor some of its programmes and teaching to the top students, or give scholarships aimed at top students, or it can target the weaker students. In either case, it has to offer something to get students to give up their place at the elite university. For example, if the regular university targets first-class students with scholarships and enhanced teaching programmes, or particularly innovative and attractive courses, the first-class students with a low value v will be attracted, while the high value V students will remain at the elite university.

We now consider whether the regular university would target the first-class or the second-class students under the Browne regime. Suppose that the regular university seeks to 'poach' 100 students back from the elite university. If it targets second-class students, and the elite university wants to keep those students, the elite university has to improve its offering to second-class students in response, incurring those extra costs for all second-class students – that is, for 500 students. The reason is that the elite university doesn't know which of its intake is at risk of defecting to the regular university. Suppose instead that the regular university targets first-class students. Then the elite university has to offer an improved programme to all its first-class students – that is 1000 students and this is likely to be particularly expensive because the incentives the regular university would have to offer to attract first-class students would be higher than those for second-class students. Perhaps surprisingly, the regular university can more effectively 'poach' 100 first-class students than 100 second-class students since the costs to the elite university in retaining those students is higher.

This argument held as well in the pre-Browne environment, and we discussed the competition for good students in that context. The potential difference is that those students are now vital to the financial – as well as academic – well-being of the institution. Even with scholarships, these students will bring up the numbers and help to cover the fixed costs at the regular university, as well as raising the academic standards and reputation of the university.

We have gone through this example on the assumption that the normal fee went up, following Browne to £6000. A higher fee level of £9000, in itself, might have had additional negative effects on competition. Some second-class students, admitted to the regular university and not the elite university, might decide that university didn't pay. In that case, the university might focus on the need to keep these students, rather than try to increase the academic strength of its programmes to bring in some top students. Additionally, as we shall argue in the next chapter, £9000 fees meant that high levels of income flowed into the university automatically. Some managements might opt for an 'easy life' and allow student numbers to drift lower, knowing that income would continue to remain at a high level.

Uncapped student numbers

In the event, the government not only allowed higher fees but it also uncapped the number of students, both at institutional and at sector levels. We argue that this had a disastrous effect, creating 'markets without competition'. The argument is simple. As with Browne, the elite university can increase its intake up to its capacity level. But now, the regular university can just admit more second-class students. It does not need to 'poach' from the elite university by offering better programmes and environment. Further, the university shifts from designing new programmes that will appeal to attracting better students, and instead aims at recruiting more weaker students. As we will argue later, the effect was compounded by the design of the contingent loan system. The subsidies are directed at the weak student enrolling on a poorly-designed and delivered programme. That student is likely to have the loan written off when their income fails to exceed the current baseline for repayment of £25,000.

In our example above, the universities might simply move to student numbers as shown in Table 3.3, provided there are sufficient weaker students willing to enrol. In the full system, rather than our two-university model, this has a ripple effect down the pecking order, where each university takes the better students from the next university below it in the hierarchy.

Table 3.3: Uncapped student numbers in the high fee regime

	Elite university	Regular university
First-class student – strongly prefers elite university	800	0
First-class student – weakly prefers elite university	200	0
Second-class student – strongly prefers elite university	400	800
Second-class student – weakly prefers elite university	100	200

The potential constraint on this process is attracting second-class students to the regular university. They need to gain a value, through employability or other factors, that makes it sensible to attend at all and incur the high fees and maintenance costs. This is another point at which the sustainability of current university strategies can be called into question – numerous universities entered the new funding regime with high reputations, but these can be eroded over time if the university makes little effort to maintain standards. If grade inflation devalues the worth of a degree, students may rationally decide not to incur the costs but to enter the job market directly.

Instead of competing for the best students, the regular university now focuses on attracting the marginal, weaker students. The government had anticipated (against all evidence) that the university might offer lower fees to make the proposition viable for these students who gain a lower value from gaining a second-class degree from the regular university. While maintaining the full £9000 fee as a perception of quality, some have in practice offered generous bursaries and scholarships as a way of implicitly cutting fees to lower the cost and improve the calculation facing the student (paid for by those students not in receipt of these incentives). Alternatively, it might be hoped that the university can attract these more marginal students by offering educational support, so that students with relatively weak preparation in some areas such as mathematics can be given intensive tutorial programmes to bring them up to speed.

It is, however, the job of the economist to be cynical, and observe that the university can instead 'compete' at zero cost through grade inflation and a lowering of the entry tariff. The ill-prepared student can be assisted through progression requirements by allowing multiple re-sits offered not a year later, as was the traditional option, but at the end of the summer. Marking can be easier, with more continuous assessment for credit. The risk of failure can be attenuated, and higher degree results than previously expected can be awarded. It is a fault in the design of the system that it encourages easier progression and grade inflation.

In some ways, universities had already dealt with this situation with overseas students. Fees and numbers had been uncapped for some years, and overseas students were charged double or more in fees compared to Home and European Union students. From some countries with the same A-level tradition as the UK, the entry qualifications of each applicant could be judged in the same way as for a home student. Students from some other countries presented a well-established Baccalaureate. But students from other large markets for an English university had more opaque qualifications that were less easy to judge. Maintaining progression standards and basing assessment predominantly upon anonymous written examinations, the outcome was that failure rates were relatively high. A university wishing to bring down non-progression could provide tutoring or other support to students. This is expensive compared to the alternative of weakening progression requirements and allowing grade inflation.

On the other hand, real educational support and improvements to the teaching programme are more sustainable over the long-term. Grade inflation in a university runs the risk of coming undone when it hits the economist's concept of 'rational expectations'. If a university has a good student and a weak student, and gives them both a first-class degree, a prospective employer reckons that an applicant with a first from that university has a 50 per cent chance of being a sound prospect and a 50 per cent chance of being weak. The employer can only learn a limited amount in a job interview, and has to rely upon the certification from the university. If the recruit doesn't pan out, the employer can dismiss them during probation, but that has been a costly exercise. Given the choice, the employer would rather recruit from a university where a 'first' continued to maintain its value.

Under 'rational expectations', you cannot hope to fool the market for an extended period of time. In the finance literature, distinction is made between 'strong', 'semi-strong' and 'weak' market efficiency. 'Strong efficiency' occurs if market prices reflect all information, whether publicly available or not. In the university context, this would require potential applicants and their potential employers to know exactly what is happening internally in each university. This is usually considered an unrealistic assumption. 'Semi-strong' requires only that publicly available information is fully incorporated. League tables abound but have surprising constituent elements. Awarding a higher percentage of 'good degrees', for a given intake, is viewed as a positive measure of 'value added' rather than a negative measure of grade inflation. It is unlikely however that major employers are fooled in this way. There appears to be some sort of cognitive dissonance in the way some universities present themselves. They espouse the £9000 fee as an indication of quality, but then inflate degree classes, lower real entry tariffs and, more recently, we have seen a dramatic increase in unconditional offers, all of which convey the opposite impression.

Over time, markets adjust to provide the information needed by consumers. A natural effect of grade inflation is to encourage other signals of quality. The Russell Group has been hugely successful as a marketing tool. If grade inflation means that in general an upper second degree is no longer a clear signal of high effort and ability, then the student who is confident of getting a good degree should make every possible effort to be admitted to a Russell Group university, and have that signal the student's ability. This has the further adverse effect of judging ability by measures applied at entry, thus reflecting prior circumstances and having a negative effect on participation from less advantaged groups.

These problems are likely to grow over time without significant policy intervention. The expansion to date of the top universities has been extremely high relative to others, but has still been relatively constrained compared to the demand for places. The elite universities – probably not accidentally – are generally in particularly favourable settings. There is limited room for expansion in central Oxford and Cambridge, and in the high property cost areas of central London where Imperial, the LSE and UCL are located. But the incentives to expansion are so great that, for example, UCL is currently planning to create what is essentially a new, full-scale university in Stratford, East London. In the first instance, this will have 4000 students. Imperial is developing a new campus in White City in West London. The students who go to these institutions would otherwise likely have gone to the next tier of London universities, who will subsequently have considerably more difficulty in recruiting students in the future. On the other hand, by taking more students the elite universities may lose some of their marketing edge by making themselves less exclusive.

Restoring competition

We will argue that caps should be put back on individual universities, at least at the top of the hierarchy. Other universities need room to breathe and compete for good students. Oxbridge, the LSE, Imperial and UCL will survive with realistic caps and may in fact prosper even more healthily. For other universities, competition has to be restored, possibly by adopting sector-wide caps as proposed by Browne. Alternatively, it is possible, perhaps likely that overall sector numbers will drop of their own accord given current figures on graduate employment, and universities below the top will have to compete for these limited numbers of applicants. Whether overall numbers become capped by policy or by demand, if the elite universities are allowed unfettered expansion, some other universities may become unviable and have to close. While bankruptcy is an integral part of unfettered competition, careful thought has to be given in advance on the role in the higher education sector. This is relevant in English universities which have built up cost bases in the last few years on the assumption that high fees and uncapped numbers would persist indefinitely.

The figure of 50 per cent participation has become an overall target for the sector, without a clear evidentiary basis, let alone the more recent uncapped policy. We have some scepticism that the arbitrary 50 per cent target for university participation is necessarily warranted. Alternatives including apprenticeships and further education should be available for students, along with vocational programmes, perhaps at private providers. Overall participation rates have become confounded with issues of widening participation across social classes and ethnic backgrounds. It is often assumed with no evidence that the marginal student must be from a less advantaged group (and conversely that privileged groups are not interested in anything but academically focused courses), and this assumption lies to a certain extent behind the relative over-representation in the less prestigious universities. We will discuss widening participation in Chapter Six, but our views and policy proposals are based on the idea that individuals from less advantaged backgrounds should be represented proportionately throughout the system. The issue of overall participation rates, and representative rates for different groups, are logically separate. For that reason, we don't see an overall cap – as proposed by Browne – as necessarily entailing less diversity in English universities.

4

Stakeholders and Expenditures

English universities are private charities that receive substantial public funding. For most institutions, this makes up the bulk of their income. Public funding comes through a buffer, given the acknowledged need to protect the independence of the individual university. This is partly a matter of efficiency – it is unhelpful to have the government of the day unduly micro-manage a university. It is also, however, a recognition of the special importance of protecting academic freedom and free speech, for both staff and students. It is ironic that the government has simultaneously issued the Prevent Duty on universities and has raised concerns about limitations to free speech on campus.

Nonetheless, the taxpayer has a right – through the government of the day – to have university expenditure reflect the taxpayers' priorities. Sometimes, the majority of academics will be supportive, as with the 'public sector equality duty' applicable to UK universities and the corresponding 'affirmative action' programmes in the US. In other cases, the priorities may not be the ones that would be chosen by the university. The taxpayer has a right, for example, to emphasise STEM (Science, Technology, Engineering and Mathematics) degrees, or instead to wish to encourage Arts degrees.

The funding authorities, independently or following government directives, set up the framework for accessing state support. The 2011 policy switched most subsidy from a block teaching grant, plus fees at £3000, to student fees of £9000 financed through the contingent loan system and limited grant to support some subject areas. Since the previous block teaching grant averaged out in the vicinity of £3000 per student, this is a substantial increase in funding. It is also a significant shift in how funding flows from the taxpayer to the university. The idea is that the student will have impact as a consumer, and that degree offerings and the quality of provision will be attuned to the market for students.

In the previous chapter, we discussed why the specific mechanisms set up were inefficient and led to less competition based on quality, not more. Here we talk more about the general level of the increase in funding, and why it also – perhaps surprisingly – had a perverse effect. Somewhat paradoxically, the increase in funding was too generous and removed the financial threat that serves as a constraint on non-profits. An analogy is with fire insurance. If there is full fire insurance with no requirement for safeguards, the owner of the property will not invest sufficiently in measures to avoid fires and put them out quickly. For a university, if the university is always at the margin where – with bad luck or bad management – it might just go bankrupt, it needs to run a diversified portfolio to minimise risk. The university cannot unduly focus on Business Studies degrees for students from China, in case that specific market dries up. The university also has to avoid excessive expensive building projects leading to debt and ongoing maintenance and staffing costs. As we discuss in Chapter Five, universities have been behaving as if the current 'golden days' of funding and low interest rates will continue for ever. This leaves the government with a real issue of potential bankruptcies if student fees are cut or student numbers drop without alternative ways for universities to make up the lost revenue. We take that up in the final chapter.

To examine the issues of non-profit behaviour, we distinguish between how a profit-maximising firm operates, and how a charity such as a university would operate. Put simply, a profit-maximising firm owes its duty to the shareholders, who have a right to the surplus generated by the firm, the profits. A non-profit, in contrast, can divide the surplus according to the preferences of its different stakeholders. This means that, for the non-profit, the outcome very much depends upon the relative bargaining strength of the different stakeholders. In structuring the university decision-making process, the taxpayer has an interest in giving the most power to the stakeholders who will most – in following their own preferences

– reflect the preferences of the public. But, since the taxpayer's preferences will not align entirely with any of the stakeholders, the optimal set-up of a university decision-making structure is to involve all the stakeholders with appropriate levels of power and influence.

Profit-maximising firms

A profit-maximising firm has a clearly defined objective. It nonetheless is constrained by the need to purchase its inputs, including labour, and to sell its products. It cannot arbitrarily determine the wages it wants to pay or the price it can get for its products. Further, the owners of the shares in the firm – unless they manage the firm themselves – need to hire managers to carry out their wishes. This leads to the 'principal–agent' problem. The managers of the firm will substitute their own preferences for those of the shareholders to the extent that they can get away with it. They may not put in much effort, they may try to extract as much cash as possible for themselves. One approach to mitigate the problem is to offer managers compensation packages that include deferred share options. In principle, the manager has a stake in the future of the firm, and therefore is more likely to be attuned to the interests of the shareholders. Nonetheless, the manager will have a limited horizon, and may engage in short-termism, where the manager takes actions that are good for apparent performance today but at the expense of the future.

The push to introducing markets for everything is based on some efficiency results in economics. Under a set of assumptions, perfect markets are efficient. They produce the right products in the right quantities. If one ignored the issue of all the assumptions, there would be a logic in setting up universities to mimic the behaviour of profit-maximising firms and letting 'the market' respond to the demands of students as consumers. The role of the government would be to target subsidies and redistribution of income and wealth following the policies of the day. In principle, if universities were all profit-maximising, a government wanting to encourage STEM subjects would offer a subsidy to those courses. If the government was concerned about *ex post* income distribution, it could set in place a contingent repayment loan scheme. To that extent, the market policies of the 2011 reforms are intellectually consistent. Once the government sets these features in place, it should simply step aside and play little further role. That is where the government has been inconsistent.

Too often, policy makers take the efficiency of markets or quasi-markets as a given, neglecting the all-important phrase 'Under a set of assumptions'. In practice, the assumptions are quite demanding, and a perfect market – and consequently full efficiency – never occurs. It is why policy sometimes avoids markets (as in the NHS), and often calls for regulation of one form or another. Since regulation brings its own inefficiencies, it is usually a case of muddling through and doing the best we can.

There are two assumptions in particular that we want to highlight in the case of universities. One is the issue of externalities, and – in particular – network externalities. We would confidently advise a student to choose the bronze Teaching Excellence Framework (TEF) LSE over a gold TEF lower-ranked university. This is not because we dispute that teaching in some sense (but perhaps not in the most important senses) is better at the gold TEF university than at the LSE. Nor is it just to do with the prestige of the LSE degree and the consequences for employability, though those are real. The major reason for going to the LSE is that one will interact with other extremely good students. That will have a positive impact on your own education. In the same way as you follow your friends onto Facebook and other social media websites, as a top student you would like to follow your A-level student peers to university.

The problem is that there can be 'lock-in' effects. The Russell Group of universities have become a dominant block to the point where other good universities cannot compete. Good students go to the Russell Group universities because other good students go there and schools encourage this choice because it enhances their own prestige. We argue elsewhere for the restoration of individual university caps on student numbers, at least for the Russell Group, in order to help restore competition into the market.

The most common argument against markets in higher education is that information is asymmetric. The university is better informed about the quality of its degree offerings than is the customer. This can be both in general – the university might know that teaching on a particular course is poor – and specific – the university might know that the prospective student's mathematics background is too weak to really succeed on a programme with high mathematical content. Much of the government's effort to address the failure of the higher education market, as has been set up, has been directed to the argument that better information will resolve the market failures. We will discuss this in depth in the following chapter. While sympathetic to the asymmetric information argument, we feel that the best way for students to acquire the relevant information remains the Open Day and other visits to prospective university choices, having narrowed down their possibilities with information from their schools and from guides and websites. There is an issue with ensuring widening participation – students from all schools, not just traditionally excellent ones, need to be properly advised to be academically ambitious. We discuss this in Chapter Six in the general context of widening participation.

Universities (in common with other businesses) can seek to address information problems with marketing. This is not necessarily a bad thing. The advertising innovator David Ogilvy is quoted 'Great marketing only makes a bad product fail faster.' It is instructive to look at the headlines by which some universities market themselves. As an example, consider universities in the 1994 Group. Although disbanded in 2013, this could be viewed as the group of universities that viewed themselves as 'Russell Group in waiting' (see Table 4.1).

Table 4.1: Marketing slogans for 1994 Group universities

Birkbeck	Join London's evening university and transform your life
East Anglia	Be brilliant
Essex	Home to the brave and bold
Goldsmiths	Untold journeys
Royal Holloway	Find your why
Lancaster	University of the year 2018
Leicester	A leading UK university
Loughborough	A top ten university: number one in the world for sports subjects
SOAS	Specialising in the study of Asia, Africa and the Near and Middle East
Sussex	World-leading research and campus by the sea

We will give in the final chapter our views on alternative strategies for this group of universities, but here observe that these catch-lines range from the bemusing 'untold journeys' and 'find your why' to the uninformative 'a leading UK university'. Our suggestion follows that of Loughborough and SOAS in the sense of having a focus and ideally a theme of being the best in the country in some areas.

A misunderstanding about competitive firms lies as well in 'managerialism'. With limited exceptions – Ryanair quickly comes to mind, or the old line 'pile it high, sell it cheap' – private sector businesses thrive on developing positive relationships with their customers and their employees. A successful business relies upon satisfied customers and loyal workers. The nature of universities – long-serving academics who choose how to apply their effort and abilities, and 'customers' who will be there for three years with little opportunity to swap supplier but ideally have a lifelong relationship as alumni – means that 'managerialism' in a simple sense is not the best way to approach the running of a university. We will discuss in some depth below how we feel it best to manage a university effectively.

Non-profit firms

The mathematical problem faced by a public-sector firm is very similar to that of a private-sector firm. There is an efficient way of running the business. Just because a university is non-profit does not mean that it shouldn't control costs and ensure high quality production, just as if the university was being run as a private business. As we have just discussed, however, efficient management is about the long term. Paying low wages, cutting pensions and putting on poor courses with ill-trained casual lecturing staff, makes no sense for either a private provider or a public university.

The difference is that the public-sector institution is no longer seeking to maximise profits. As a first approximation, the non-profit can determine how to recruit and educate students in an efficient way, just as the profit-maximising university would. The non-profit, however, does not distribute the surplus to shareholders as dividends, but spends it according to the preferences of the stakeholders, roughly in proportion to the bargaining power held by each. The object of a business is to make as much profit as possible, whereas a university ideally should want to spend as much as possible to support its responsibilities for teaching and research subject to financial prudence. Both want to maximise income, universities through student income, research funding and research grants, consultancies and spin-offs and alumni donations. As a first approximation, fees of £9000 and efficient costs of £6000 per student lead to a surplus of £3000 per student to be spent. The student and the taxpayer have a right that this surplus – that they have funded – should be spent in a way that best maximises the student's and the public interest. The massive extent of the surpluses – particularly for Russell Group and elite universities – is seen in Figure 4.1.

The (obviously false) assumption of government was that some universities would not charge the maximum fee, in order to attract more students. But in any case, government no doubt thought that the surplus would be used in the first instance on improving the student experience and for widening participation, under the auspices of the Office for Fair Access (OFFA). Indeed, a university

Figure 4.1: Surpluses at universities

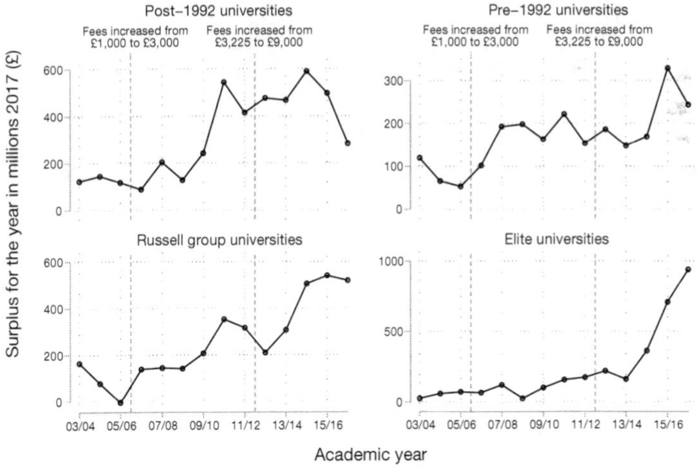

Note: HE institutions with fewer than ten students are excluded in this figure. The surplus is before property revaluations, actuarial gains/losses in respect of pension schemes and changes in the fair value of financial instruments.

Source: HESA Finance Record 2003/04–2016/17

needed to have its access plans approved by the Office in order to charge more than the £6000 basic fee, up to £9000. These plans involved all sorts of assessments, strategic plans, expected spend on access including financial support to students and self-determined targets all of which come at an administrative and opportunity cost. As we will discuss in Chapter Six, it would have been better just to have had clear targets to be set to reflect national priorities. The residual after expenditures to achieve broader access would no doubt, in the minds of the government and civil servants, have been spent on attracting and recruiting students by offering top quality programmes. In the competitive market envisaged, not all universities would have set fees at the maximum £9000 for all courses, they would have offered scholarships in addition to financial need bursaries, and they would have recruited academic staff to teach revitalised and newly designed courses. As we have discussed in the previous chapter, universities could instead just sidestep the competition and admit weaker students, competing for these weaker students with grade inflation.

For those reasons, much of the surplus could be considered as free funds to be allocated according to the preferences of the stakeholders. We consider each in turn.

Students as consumers or students as stakeholders

Students have never been unduly franchised in the university. The Student Union President typically sits on university councils, and there is a limited (if any) appearance of students on departmental boards and university senates. Student bargaining power has had more of an indirect nature, where effective teachers and administrators listen to students. There is in particular daily interaction between students and lecturers, and between students and departmental-level administrative staff. This is one of the reasons for placing a lot of decision-making at the departmental level, where the student voice can best be heard.

For individual issues, students would have a personal advisor. With a relatively low student–staff ratio, the student would be able to meet with the advisor as and when needed. The student would be able to get references. Traditionally, however, there was also a Dean of Students who was the backstop for students and a representative for their interests and concerns. A student facing hardship or other issues could go directly to the Dean of Students and gain a sympathetic ear and practical support. The Dean may also detect generic issues and serve an early warning to senior managers of matters that need attention.

At one of the American universities where one of us was a visiting teacher, each new entry class would plant a tree during induction week. The idea was that they were a part of the institution and – as the tree grew over the next several decades – their attachment to the college would take further root and grow. American universities find it particularly important to develop that long-term bond since they rely on alumni to provide donations to the university endowment, something we would like to see encouraged in UK universities for academic reasons, as much as financial ones.

It is hard to understand why it is felt to be optimal to have committees of middle-aged people sitting in a room, perhaps armed with surveys and focus group reports prepared by expensive marketing consultants, deciding what 19-year-old potential students might want. There are, in the university, thousands of students who can directly tell you what they want and how they would spend the surplus. Indeed, one of the things that students most want is to be listened to, so inviting students into the decision-making process kills two birds with one stone – it has a direct benefit in involving current students and the related benefit in learning from the relevant group how to practically implement their preferences. It also encourages students to feel valued members of the entire community.

More prosaically, having incurred debts of up to £60,000, students want a degree of value. That will be the topic of the next chapter.

Academics

Academic staff have chosen a career in the university for a number of different reasons. These are highly educated individuals, generally to PhD level, who have also demonstrated particular capability in their chosen subject. Some are in fields – Biochemistry, Physics, Information Security, Finance – where they could easily command multiples of their salaries in the private sector. Others, in fields of lesser external demand – such as History or the Arts – spend years in training and then casual employment in low-paid visiting teaching jobs, until they hope at some point to obtain a lectureship. In turn, academics gain the chance to spend their time pursuing their chosen interests in study they value and in teaching students. Successful academics put in long hours on their research and teaching, but have the advantage of flexibility in scheduling their work. They gain the trapping of professionals, with private offices.

In general, the senior managers running a university need to come from an academic career. In part, this is to avoid simplistic errors such as proposing – as Directors of Estates regularly do – that academics should share open plan offices. HR Directors wonder why academics do not regularly get their leave days approved in advance by their line manager (Head of Department) and why they are not in their offices from 9 to 5. Occasionally, they are bemused by why an academic has sent them an e-mail at 3 in the morning, since it doesn't occur to them that an academic may be doing research at that time, perhaps communicating with a co-researcher in Australia or North America.

Some academics, as in other fields of work, are not performing at 100 per cent by observable metrics. An English literature professor may not have written a book for ten years, or a lecturer in Physics may not have published a paper for the last three years. They may be working on long-term and difficult projects. They may be going through a difficult patch with their research. It does not mean that they can simply be written off. We will discuss below why universities are organised in departments, and why that is the locality for dealing with such issues. Typically, if an academic hasn't been publishing, they want to contribute in other ways. They can take up additional administrative responsibilities, such as Director of Undergraduate Studies, or additional teaching. At the university level, they can serve in numerous roles, including in the Dean of Students Office (which, as we have argued above, served a vital role in student wellbeing in the past). There are other academics who – while not publishing themselves – serve as an amazing resource for new lecturers, reading their papers and helping them on their research. In our experience, there are very few academics who don't pull their weight, in one way or another, and even fewer who don't respond positively if guided by a Head of Department.

Research and teaching

It has always been the case, and reinforced by both the Robbins and Dearing Reports, that universities have dual responsibilities for teaching and research, the latter being expressed as a critical examination and extension of existing knowledge and its transmission to the next generation. Elite, Russell and non-Russell pre-1992 universities emphasise 'research-led teaching'. It is believed that active researchers in a field are best placed to teach undergraduate as well as postgraduate students. Research-led teaching is based upon the idea that research and teaching are complementary in production. It is helpful to have a clear idea on precisely what this means. If someone is teaching six hours a week without doing research, and another continues to do six hours a week face-to-face teaching but is also doing research, the teaching done by the research/teaching member of staff will be more productive for the student than the teaching done by the non-researcher. In making this statement, we have deliberately kept the hours of teaching relatively low. If the hours of teaching rise significantly, in order to maintain research productivity the research/teaching member of staff will need to economise on teaching preparation, for example, or in marking essays and examinations. This is the sense in which – at low teaching hours – the two activities are complementary, and – as teaching hours rise – they become substitutes. It is also the case that in many subjects there is a marked symbiosis. A historian working on archive material for a forthcoming book can use this directly to inform and enthuse their teaching. In Mathematics and the Sciences, high level research is sometimes some distance away from undergraduates' understanding, but it is nevertheless the case that the general objectives of such research can be conveyed and undergraduate teaching enlivened and informed as part of a living and growing enterprise.

Consequently, while research-led teaching is a good thing – it means that the lecturer is enthusiastic and in tune with the latest developments in their subject – it is not inexpensive. It is therefore totally sensible to have some universities engaged in the research-led teaching model, with staff doing research at top international level and having their students benefit from this, while other universities are more focused on teaching. This may well be reflected in the course offerings – some courses do not need as high-level a research basis as others to be relevant and up to date.

If staff are not engaged in research at the top international level, it is more economical for them to spend more hours in teaching rather than produce research that will have little impact, although they will need to keep up to date with developments in their subject even if they are not directly contributing to them. We would argue however that the current fashion for 'teaching-focused' academics hired into predominantly research departments is a mistake. In a department which is very actively engaged in research, with an active programme of research seminars, there are positive externalities in all lecturers participating in the programme. As we have indicated, over time some staff will shift their interests from research to teaching or administration, and in that sense 'teaching-focused' staff naturally develop in a department. Furthermore recruiting young 'teaching-focused' staff, for whom, logically, there will be a higher teaching load, cuts them off from developing their own research and likely leads to an unfortunate disparity in prestige within the department. It is one of many ways in which a 'managerial' approach can be 'penny-wise and pound foolish'.

We have deliberately put our focus on 'department'. While Research Excellence Framework (REF) results show that research excellence is concentrated in the top universities, and more generally in the pre-1992 universities, each university has particular research strengths, and there are few universities that do not have research excellence in some departments. This is a perfectly sensible organisation. Some universities will have top ten departments in every subject, others will be more specialised, and some will have research excellence in a limited number of areas. This last group should find outstanding performance in other areas of the university remit, notably in teaching, particularly in areas that intrinsically do not require a research base. Each university should define its mission, but be excellent in fulfilling its mission, and supported by the funding system in accomplishing these goals.

The RAE/REF

In 1986, the first Research Assessment Exercise (RAE) was undertaken. Each unit of assessment (subject group) was assigned a score. This exercise and its successor the REF has been undertaken roughly every four to six years subsequently. Academics have generally bought into the process, which has been influential in determining the reputation of each department and university. Since the assessment was by subject group, which corresponds roughly to departments, this has further strengthened academics' focus upon their department. Although funds go to the university based upon each department's individual strength, the sums are not required to be spent on that department. Nonetheless, it is the reputational effect that is most important to academics and indeed to the university. A department that does not get the highest ranking may not greet the news with unalloyed joy, but will recognise that high ranking departments bring prestige to the whole university. In turn high ranking departments will see, albeit reluctantly, that some of the income accruing from their own success benefits the whole enterprise if used to bring up the performance elsewhere. But a management structure that encourages collegiality and 'the greater good' is essential if such behaviour is to be encouraged.

The advantage of the RAE/REF is that research is largely measurable. Each unit of assessment listed publications for each submitted member of staff. The expert panel could assess the level of contribution of each publication – it is relatively straightforward to see what is of international standing, what is of national standing, and what is relatively weak in terms of academic merit. The research environment – numbers of PhD students, grants and so on, was also considered, but again much of this is relatively easy to measure. In addition, academics tend to have a common view on the importance of research, and leading scholars served on the first and subsequent panels.

In a way, the RAE/REF became a victim of its own success. It was distorting, since it measured output in four- to six-year periods, so 'blue skies' research might be discouraged. However, not all research and teaching academics needed to be listed in each round, so a longsighted university could 'cover' for an academic who was in the midst of a cyclical lull while working on important longer-term research. The exercise clearly upped the game of academics throughout the country. But it also necessarily created a 'transfer market' of academics with strong submissions in a given RAE/REF round, driving up salaries.

There is always a problem when individuals or teams or departments produce multiple goods, and only one is readily measurable. The university, as we have discussed, produces research, teaching and what has come to be called 'impact' – public policy contributions. Research is measurable by the quality of academic publications. Good teaching, in contrast, is virtually impossible to define, much less measure. We know that teaching evaluations suffer from gender and other biases, and in any case these are popularity measures as much or more than quality of education measures. It does not take a new lecturer long to learn that giving hints on examination questions, or providing continuous assessment with high marks, has a positive impact on evaluations.

The REF is again an example where there are markets but the funding agencies shy away from competition. If the purpose of the exercise is to encourage individual and team research, then it is natural that this would be reflected in higher salaries in response to good individual and team performances. For the next REF, however, 'portability' is being limited in the sense that – should an individual leave a university either for a better opportunity or in anger and frustration – their publications are still counted in the erstwhile location. This change is explicitly designed to lower salaries as described in the Stern Report.[1]

It was felt that, by concentrating upon academic contributions of research, 'impact' – public policy – was being ignored. Therefore, in 2014, 'impact case studies' became an important part of the REF, a role to be amplified in the 2021 REF. Whether or not one thinks that public policy should be an inherent part of the evaluation of research, the point is that it is not measurable. Unlike a list of publications, there needs to be a written narrative of a 'case study'. We will argue in Chapter Five that these vague approaches to measurement, opening up the door to salesmanship, are a fundamental problem with the current quality control measures from the QAA (Quality Assurance Agency), the NSS (National Student Survey) and the TEF.

That the REF was successful also meant that resources would be shifted to research from teaching. Research was measured and rewarded. Even though research and teaching can be complementary activities, workload hours may be shifted from teaching to research if higher priority is given to research. The idea of the TEF is to balance this out. However, this fails to understand the nature of a budget constraint. One can incentivise research at the expense of teaching, or teaching at the expense of research, but one cannot incentivise both – the effects simply cancel out and one is left with only the deadweight costs of the assessment process both within and without the university. In any case, attempts to place an increased weight on teaching will merely lead to attention on measurable features such as teaching evaluations and underplay the quality that derives from teaching informed by a challenging atmosphere of research and enquiry.

What do academics want?

After this digression, we can now return to the question of how academics would have spent the windfall if they had been in control. At the research-intensive universities, and indeed at universities somewhat short of meriting that description over the whole institution (but, as we have said, still with areas of international strength), academics want to do their research. They want articles published in good journals and books published with top university and trade presses. They want to obtain research grants and do more resource-heavy research, employing research assistants and funding PhD students. They want well-resourced labs. They want to go to conferences and present their work, and to see their citation indexes go up. Depending upon the individual, they want to have PhD students and teach their specialist subject in final year undergraduate courses. The more charismatic lecturers enjoy going before large core groups of 100 or 200 and inspiring first year students.

The way to square the circle, to meet the desires for research focus but also high-quality teaching, is to hire more academic staff.

We think that it is more than a projection of our own preferences, but our view is that academics would use an increase in funding to hire more academic staff with some additional administrative support, to provide good teaching facilities and office space, and to target student numbers that would allow for a reasonably qualified intake of undergraduates and postgraduates. An increase in academic staff numbers, at junior and senior level invigorates the department, secures its future and will in any case generate more income through research grants and the REF.

How should this be managed?

The traditional managerial structure of a research-intensive university was designed to reflect the interests of the academics. The Vice Chancellor would typically be a Pro-Vice-Chancellor from another university who had a distinguished academic background but chose to remain in an administrative post.

We start from the notion that an academic's first interest is in the subject and that is nourished by an active department. It is therefore in the interests of the university as a whole to support departments as the level where true academic energy lies and where commitment to standards is best nurtured. It is at this level where the scholarship of the academic can be judged, as well as their contributions to the teaching and administration within the department. Academics will typically have closer ties to those in the same subject in other universities than to those even in cognate subjects within their own university. This allows, and indeed requires, a commitment to the quality standards within the discipline. The REF judges this on the research front, and a strong subject-based system of external examiners maintains this for teaching programmes. If there is a strong, supportive and stimulating environment, this gets out within the subject nationally and internationally, and helps in recruiting high quality staff and further building the department to the benefit of the whole university.

The Head of Department then represents these interests into the central university planning and other processes. The Dean balances the wishes of the department against those of the other departments in the faculty and represents those to the Centre. The

Dean has also to communicate back the balancing act that has been made with other Deans. The Deans as a group play a critical role in formulating the overall plan and decision making at the university senate, consulting with and carrying the academic community in development and support of the plan. The Heads also meet together to discuss institutional level issues, not least because it reinforces their value as the players on the real field of action and helps them to understand differing views from subject to subject within the university. Finally, it is important that Heads have direct access to the Vice Chancellor to resolve any urgent problems or where the department needs particular assistance.

In 'matrix management', the Pro-Vice Chancellors have the role of being champions for their part of the strategy (research, teaching, staffing, estates or other issues). They act orthogonally to the Deans expressing needs for the prosecution of their responsibilities and stimulating and monitoring progress across all departments. Importantly, these individuals need to have the academic standing that is the main currency of status within the university. This is important to validate that the mission of the institution is academic and not focused, for example, on profit-and-loss accounts.

Viewed as a pyramid where the real action is of necessity occurring at departmental level, this is a model where information flows upwards, with senior managers having the role of quality control and integration of the needs of the units. Micro-management is rightly criticised as a style in almost all contexts, but is particularly problematic in the university because of the primary identification of academics with their subject and department. The ability to judge quickly diminishes as one moves away from the scene of the real action. This is one of the reasons why the REF has proved so powerful – it is senior academics in the subject area from other universities that are judging the academics in that subject within the current institution. It is also why the external system of evaluation – as discussed in the next chapter – is so important.

We are not sure why 'managerialism' – top-down approaches to running a university – have become prevalent at just the time when the large inflows of funding occurred. But the effects are predictable in that the preferences of managers – both academic and non-academic – would become dominant in the allocation of the new resources. When the shift to uncapped, high-fee student numbers was announced, two of the authors were at lunch with an eminent visiting American academic. He confidently predicted that, when administrators decided how to spend the funds, it would be in large building programmes. In some ways, this is not surprising – a new building is literally a concrete achievement, visible to all, opened by the Queen or another dignitary. Building academic programmes, raising standards of intake gradually over the years, setting up research centres and gaining external funding, recruiting top quality staff to raise outcomes in the next and subsequent REFs, are all long-term projects. For academics with a 20-year horizon at the institution, this is a meaningful investment that raises their standing nationally and internationally with their subject peers. For a Chief Operating Officer seeking a new post at a larger university, these slow steps may be of less interest.

The governing body, alumni and donors

Traditionally, governing bodies included people with experience and expertise not readily available within the university in order to provide advice and reassure the public that the place was well governed. They did not see their role as running the place or determining academic policy. We therefore do not see the governing body as being a substitute for academic governance of the institution. The restoration of the power of university senates, of academic participation on major university decision-making committees and structures, seems to us to be the way to restore balance in the university. In part, this is because governing bodies are typically not academically focused but contain successful business people and professionals from law and public service bringing their own expertise. They have a rightful role in ensuring a combination of prudence and entrepreneurship, and we will as we approach policy be asking universities to become much more centres of academic entrepreneurship rather than engaging in unimaginative copycat behaviour. The governing body should be there giving an overview, giving reassurance to the public that money is well spent and stepping in on those rare occasions when it is necessary, to guide their institution towards the excellence we are seeking.

More generally, their role is to keep asking hard questions, but not to seek to manage.

In the US system, there are other important stakeholders, alumni and (often the same group) donors to the university. Alumni represent a largely altruistic group that is seeking the best for their institution. They are there to visit and give talks and advice to students, to help them in internships and placements, and to provide general support to the institution. We earlier gave the example of the American university where each class plants a tree to make a lifelong commitment. We think that that can only be to the good of the institution. That alumni can then be asked, and often volunteer, to contribute to projects and scholarships, strikes us as a further benefit.

Both the UK and the US experience with large donors shows that there are tensions in relying upon that as a source of finance. It is often directed at building projects (not necessarily a top priority for the university) with the donor's name on the building (which is, we suppose, better than using the surplus from student fees in this way), or in pet projects of the donor. And there are occasional bad experiences when a generous donation comes from a controversial source. A university can quickly go broke from too many donations tied to particular activities, which are not necessarily aligned with the real priorities, rather than general funds. It may be, however, that part of the reluctance in the UK to gain donor finance has to do with creating another, powerful group of stakeholders. We have indicated that, for a non-profit where no one group of stakeholders fully represents the taxpayer's interest in providing the bulk of funding, increasing the number and power of other stakeholders may nonetheless be a good.

We raised near the beginning of this chapter the principal–agent problem in profit-maximising firms. This becomes even more pronounced in non-profits. The funders – in UK universities, primarily the taxpayer and now the student through fees – need universities to empower stakeholders who are most likely to carry out the preferences of those paying the bills. The traditional university structure – putting the academics at the centre of the decision-making process – was largely efficient. 'Managerialism' does not work in the long run even in the private sector. The rise in managerialism in universities occurred in conjunction with the large surpluses generated by the increase in upfront taxpayer funding for teaching. It is in the nature of a non-profit that the dominant stakeholders would spend those funds following their preferences. When we come to policies in the final chapter, our proposals do not involve additional funding. It does not seem right that the sector should be able to go to the taxpayer for still more funding, which we feel can be better directed elsewhere in education. Instead, new policies should shift incentives and structures to better match the preferences stated by government for greater 'value for money', quality of education and widening participation. Nonetheless, policymakers will still need to balance the current desire of students for lower fees and the need to provide sufficient funding for universities to conduct their mission and – in the light of an increase in the cost base over the last few years due to building programmes – remain solvent. Alumni and other donors can help square the circle, as is the case in US universities.

English universities have started to take the issue of alumni and other donations on board, but with limited exceptions (primarily the elite universities) have set out modest ambitions. The main objective should be – as in the US system – to get as many alumni as possible to contribute, even if the sums are relatively small. Someone starting off their career can give a small annual donation of £20, and it should be welcomed by the institution. A modest-sized university producing 3000 graduates a year has the potential, in this way, to generate £3.3 million after ten years and £12.6 million after 20 years. Of course not every graduate would join the scheme but some would commit more than £20 a year as their careers developed, and once into the habit highly successful graduates may become significant donors.

The point is that there is great potential for raising additional funds but, perhaps even more importantly, the continuing donation scheme would depend for its success on the student experience and therefore on the commitment of all staff having a direct impact on the quality of the student experience. To maintain the commitment of alumni into the future, they would have to have not only these memories of a good experience but pride in their university through its continuing commitment to its reputation and standards. The success of the scheme would require that the standard and value of the degree remained high and the university recruited academics of the highest quality, by a halo effect further burnishing the value to the alumni and the attractiveness of the university to potential applicants. This positive incentive to all staff would be healthier and more effective than visits from inspectors and QAA reports.

We have repeated several times the irony of how those who profess greatest belief in applying markets to universities don't grasp the possibilities for real competitive practices. Suppose that a university depended upon alumni donations in order to represent the balance between a reasonably well-funded institution and one that has difficulty paying the light bill each month. The university has a strong incentive to ensure that students feel that they have got 'value for money' and a valuable degree, that their first- or second- class degree has not suffered from grade inflation so that they can use it to validate their accomplishments to a potential employer, and that they participated fully as a valued member of the university community.

5

Expanding Numbers and Maintaining Standards

The substantial increase in per student funding that came with the new fees and funding policy was predicated on increased and widening participation in universities. We have questioned the 50 per cent target, particularly given evidence that graduates are now frequently being placed in non-graduate jobs.[1] Other forms of higher and further education, and apprenticeships, are valuable alternatives to university, depending upon students' interests and abilities. In any case, we feel strongly that expansion should not be a reason for lowering standards, particularly under policies which provided more than sufficient additional unit of resource – if wisely used – to provide extra support for non-traditional students. Indeed, that was the policy *quid pro quo* for a university being allowed to raise fees beyond the base £6000 up to £9000.

We have already raised our concerns that the top universities simply cream off more of the best students in general and meet widening participation objectives by taking the best non-traditional applicants, without engaging in sufficient outreach to widen the pool. As we move through the hierarchy, both for the existential need to attract more students and the more honourable motive to offer better life chances, universities lower down the league tables may feel they have to offer low entry requirements. It is doubtful whether, however committed and talented their teaching may be, they will be able to bring students to the same level and on similar courses after three years as those admitted to the top universities.

For these reasons, if we are to maintain high standards throughout the system, we feel that the diversity of institutions has to be kept in mind. It may be that we are moving toward the varied post-compulsory offering that Dearing advocated but at the price that the term 'university' now has a wider meaning. This is not to say that those universities with world class researchers and courses which make the highest intellectual demands are making a more valuable contribution. It is not so much a question of 'better' or 'worse' but different. Quantum Physics is not available everywhere and neither should it be, but that is not to say that less academically demanding courses and those that do not require research activity within the department are not important – to the individual and to society – and they may open up opportunities for further study to those wanting it and whose potential is revealed.

Maintaining standards in a diverse system

Before 1992, diversity was represented more clearly and the university and polytechnic sectors had their own methods for ensuring standards. The question is how to maintain standards in an even more diverse system of institutions with the same name ('university') and regulatory frameworks. The key tool in ensuring standards has been the external examiner system, which has been in place for universities for nearly 100 years. It seeks to reassure the public that degrees awarded by approved institutions reach a common standard. We have observed that universities that offer under-prepared students a first-rate experience and open opportunities and courses that would not otherwise be available are unlikely to be able to bring them to the same 'standard' as longstanding universities with highly qualified applicants. Those universities that offer chances to those with lower formal qualifications often offer courses in subjects not widely available and for which comparison of standards is not easy. For these reasons, the guidance for external examiners is that it is their duty to ensure consistent standards of degrees in their subject *across comparable institutions*.

A student graduates from University X with a degree of classification C in subject S. A potential employer does not require that the methodology for maintaining standards across the sector achieves the same classification of degrees across institutions with different missions. A first from Oxford in Physics, where the student has been well-prepared before coming to university and is being taught by international scholars winning Nobel prizes in the best possible equipped laboratories, can and probably should mean something different from someone getting a first in more applied Physics at a largely non-research department in a less elite university. The important thing is that the degree and its classification should be understood and valued by potential employers. Depending upon the job, employers may favour the non-Oxford degree if they can be assured that the degree means what it says.

From our discussion in Chapter Three, it can be seen that there has been substantial grade inflation throughout the sector and this has run the danger of devaluing degrees except at the very top institutions (where reputation trumps grade inflation). It seems unlikely that firsts, once awarded for truly exceptional performance, can now legitimately be given to so many. However, in the current atmosphere of students as customers more firsts seem to be a 'good thing'. The preservation of the integrity of degrees and the ending of grade inflation has not attracted so much attention within the sector as the perceived quality of student experience reported in the NSS (National Student Survey) and the Teaching Excellence Framework (TEF).

Even, however, in a world where students are perceived as customers and student immediate satisfaction is deemed to be of paramount importance, at the end of the day the student wants a credible degree to show to employers. This is why students are desperate to attend a Russell Group university and obtain that label on their degree certificate, whether or not it is the right course for them. We argue that non-Russell universities have the most to gain from restoration of confidence in the awarding and classification of degrees, even if they will need to spend considerable sums in the short run to re-focus their efforts on the quality of education, notably by tightening admission standards and hiring more academics.

Process or performance

We began this book by quoting from the National Audit Office (NAO), which describes a sector in crisis, with the strong majority of students finding poor 'value for money'. The government has raised the issue of rampant grade inflation. Inflation by definition is a devaluation of the currency in question, in this case the standard of degrees.

The Quality Assurance Agency (QAA) has responsibility for ensuring quality and standards in teaching. As we commented in Chapter Two its history has not been untroubled but, after reforms, it continues as an independent body offering advice to the Office for Students (OfS). A benign, indeed rosy picture is painted by the QAA. In its 2015/16 Higher Education Review, it observes that 'As a result of this work, the public can have confidence in the standards and quality of UK higher education.' Of the higher education institutions reviewed, 100 per cent received all positive outcomes, with 25 per cent receiving commendations.

How can they both be right? The answer is that the QAA looks predominantly at process, and the NAO looks at outcomes. Further, the QAA process is moderated by the institution being able to present its materials and its case. Typically, if one goes to see a Jackson Pollock exhibition, there is a film short of the artist engaged in making a drip painting. The film is informative and entertaining, and no doubt played a role in developing the career and marketing of Pollock's work. It helps to make the argument that Pollock was engaged in an artistic act, although the recent reported sale of a Pollock painting for $140 million probably has little to do with that film, and more to do with the inherent valuation placed by the purchaser on the painting. In the same way, the winner at Wimbledon is not determined by an inspection and evaluation of training programmes or past form, but by performance on the day. The commentators might well observe that Andy Murray was playing particularly elegant shots, but that would not determine who went home with the trophy and the winner's cheque.

If one wanted to judge the standards of a UK university, one could randomly choose students in each major subject area with stipulated entry A-level grades, set them a common subject examination written by externals and graded by externals who did not know which university was involved, compare the examination results to their final degree results, and come to a conclusion. This was once the system operated by the University of London for the constituent colleges, reinforced by a common degree ceremony held in the Albert Hall. Today, however, it is clearly not a feasible solution over the entire university sector.

External examiners

Or is it? One could argue that the last paragraph is, at least in essence, in the spirit of the external examiner system. Clearly, grade inflation is reflective of the reality that this system is not ensuring that historical standards are maintained in the examination and marking process. The Higher Education Academy (HEA) has been engaged in a HEFCE (Higher Education Funding Council for England) funded contract on the subject of maintaining degree standards. Its primary work to date has been to develop a training programme (which can be accessed online) for external examiners, with further work on the calibration of academic standards through degree algorithms. The HEA emphasises that the programme is 'sector-led and sector-owned'.

Vice Chancellors and pro-Vice Chancellors might be saints, but it is a first principle of regulation that it cannot be 'sector-led and sector-owned' since the precise purpose is to challenge the sector. University managements – the sector – can and should be consulted, as should the other stakeholders we have described in Chapter Four. It may be the case that university managers all feel that the grade inflation must be stopped and will support stringent actions. In that scenario, the only impediment is that it cannot be done unilaterally. Alternatively, managers of different universities may have different interests. The Russell Group might well regret grade inflation, while other universities may (misguidedly, in our view) see it as their best way to compete. On the principle that the taxpayer and the student are entitled to 'value for money', whether or not there is consensus from the sector is of minimal interest.

What has gone wrong with the external examiner system? It is ironic that those who believe in markets have not turned to the most obvious factor, the lack of commensurate remuneration (in either financial or other forms) for the task.

We have discussed in Chapter Four that much of what academics do is not directly remunerated. Being an external assessor for senior posts, for example, is typically not remunerated, nor is refereeing for articles in even commercial press journals or grant evaluations for the research councils. These are seen as contributing to the health of the discipline. But external examiner duties are onerous. Examining a PhD will typically take more than a day (and sometimes several days) to read the PhD and prepare for the oral examination, which itself will involve travel and therefore typically take another day. The reports must be agreed with follow-ups for minor revisions or for further submissions of more extensive changes. The University of Nottingham helpfully has put its normal fees for externals on its website. The remuneration for being an external examiner on a PhD is £210. In contrast, universities typically charge consultancy fees for professors at about £400–£600 a day, or more.

Senior academics view the PhD as fundamentally important to nurturing and developing the next generation of researchers. In that sense, the reward is a notional honorarium and could be supplemented by a nice dinner with colleagues at the other university. We have discussed how academics are focused upon their subject area, and owe their loyalties to their discipline, so are willing to undertake these tasks with minimal or no financial reward.

Moving to the MSc, that is less the case. In terms of career development, it is the sort of thing a Senior Lecturer might do to enhance their case for being promoted to Reader or Professor. An MSc with 10–30 students takes a lot of work. The external needs to go over the draft examination papers and suggest changes. The external gets a sample of the scripts to see if the overall marks given internally are appropriately matched to discipline standards. The external then attends the sub-board on the day to be involved in the discussions. At Nottingham, for an MSc with 20 students, the remuneration is £600.

When we turn to undergraduates, an external for the degree receives £200 plus £6 per student. The duties are similar to those of the MSc, but there will be considerably more papers for the different course options. There is little professional kudos for doing undergraduate external examining. It is unlikely that a senior professor would be willing to undertake this task in the current environment.

Rather than the QAA setting up online or other training for less experienced academics to serve as externals and for developing benchmarks for degrees and subjects as described below, we would argue that there needs to be a core of senior professors leading the process. As with other parts of our job, less experienced academics should work in tandem with more senior ones. Externals could be appointed centrally from a list and report – in addition to the university – to a central monitoring group. Remuneration has to increase (in many cases, it has been unchanged for decades), but even 'market rates for the job' are unlikely alone to attract senior academics. We need to return to a system where academics are motivated by obligations and responsibilities to their subject.

Further, as was traditionally the case, the external has to be the 'decider'. The courtesy of turning to the external during the examination sub-board and saying to them 'It is your decision' has an impact of reminding everyone that there are objective standards and it is the role of the external to enforce them. That external control may mean that half the students on the MSc fail in a given year if the intake was poor and the teaching weak. That possibility would keep the department and university focused upon not letting academic standards slip. This external influence is strengthened with the academic standing of the external, but weakened if the external examiner is relatively junior in experience to the internal members of the board.

The future role of the QAA, NSS and TEF

Our view is that the QAA, NSS and TEF are not assessing and measuring what needs to be measured. It is hard to see the value, for example, in a QAA Quality Code that describes a 'bachelor's degree with honours' as being awarded to 'students who have demonstrated':[2]

- a systematic understanding of key aspects of their field of study;
- an ability to deploy accurately established techniques;

- conceptual understanding;
- an appreciation of the uncertainty, ambiguity and limits of knowledge;
- the ability to manage their own learning.

Anyone in the sector should have a concept of a bachelor's degree, and this general sort of specification does not assist in determining the value of any given degree. It seems almost designed for an alien arriving from Mars, in the unlikely event that – despite their mastery of space travel – they do not have a university sector.

The NSS

A major tool for the QAA's assessment policy is the NSS. Asking students about their experience is consistent with pressures to regard the student as a customer paying for a service. Setting aside the obvious fact that the student as 'customer' is not always 'right' and has to be pushed and sometimes made to feel uncomfortable if they are to realise their full potential, some issues of methodology have to be addressed. First, the questions asked are subjective. There is no baseline against which students can make a judgement. So, for example, one of the questions is 'The timetable works for me: grade 1–5'. What does this mean? No lectures before 10am? Or 'I had the right opportunities to provide feedback on my courses: grade 1–5'. What is 'right'? Perhaps it would be better to ask, for example, 'Was your timetable made clear?' (Yes or No). Or 'Was it made clear what courses would be available to you on the programme to which you were admitted?' (Yes or No). 'Were the courses actually available?' (Yes or No). In other words, questions requiring a 'yes or no' response would at least stand a chance of being less subjective. In any case, while it may be useful for a university to ask the NSS sort of 'consumer feedback' questions of its students for its own use, they are of little objective value for external assessments of quality. If the government objective is to impose market disciplines on universities it should ask itself why customer feedback at, say, John Lewis, is left to the company and not imposed by a regulatory agency.

It might seem surprising that in practice the bulk of university NSS scores lie in very high percentiles, the 90s or 80s. Speaking with students, they make clear that – in filling out the NSS – they are guided by a perceived need to 'talk up' their university. They feel that their degree would lose value if their university received poor scores. In the National Union of Students boycott of the 2017 NSS, notable impacts (in terms of lowering the response rate to the point where the university was not listed in results tables) occurred at Cambridge, Oxford and other top universities, where students might feel more secure that the NSS was irrelevant to the standing of their degree.

A deeper question arises in the context of expectations of the university experience. The emphasis traditionally is on students being responsible for their own development with sympathetic and expert guidance from their teachers rather than being taught more in the way they have probably experienced at school. This comes as a surprise to some students and this important shift in perspective is impeded by the encouragement for students to regard themselves as customers wanting results commensurate with the fees they have paid.

The TEF

The TEF has been introduced with the object of publishing data to inform student choice. It is also intended to be a counterbalance to the REF which, some have argued, has resulted in too much emphasis being put on research to the detriment of teaching and has figured in league tables to the disadvantage of those universities which do not see their mission as developing leading edge research.

TEF is based on the NSS and a set of metrics, with written submissions from universities to be analysed by panels. The guidance notes to universities as to how the system will work and how to make submissions runs to 64 pages. (How many pages do TEF staff have to read to cover the whole sector?) The results of the analysis of applications are ratings of Gold, Silver or Bronze. It is envisaged that the outcomes may in the future determine whether universities can charge higher fees.

We have argued that measurement of outcomes and attention to standards is more objective and useful than an inspection of process. We view the written submissions to TEF as a classic case of marking essay submissions from senior administrators, something we see as having little positive impact on the quality of education for our students. Central costs will be of the order of £500,000 and preparation of submissions will no doubt lead to extra administration costs within universities. Not only will this, ironically, drain funds away from the core activity of teaching that it is meant to improve but will add further to the administrative emphasis resulting from regulation. This in turn leads to an implicit reorganisation of how a university operates. The top-down approach is fuelling an unhelpful gulf between academic and central administrative staff who are in danger of being seen as a police force rather than colleagues sharing the same endeavour.

The OfS consider that the TEF awards will settle down to roughly 20 per cent Gold, 50–60 per cent Silver and 20–30 per cent Bronze. This seems extraordinary. If the objective is to improve standards of teaching then surely an aim should be 100 per cent Gold. The current expectation is that 20–30 per cent will not be up to scratch. Not a very ambitious target and not one which will do much good to the perception overseas. How is a prospective student supposed to interpret the results? If TEF is measuring teaching and learning accurately, why should a student ever go to a 'Bronze' university or subject within a university? Alternatively, if the TEF is not an accurate measure of the educational quality of an institution, why are we engaging in the expense and distortions associated with TEF?

There are many metrics already available through HESA (Higher Education Statistics Agency) and more are being developed on, for example, graduate employment and earnings. Participation data (on social background and ethnicity) would be easily available if means testing of fees and maintenance grants was adopted. With proper attention to the standards of qualifications awarded, data on results and drop-out compared with entry qualifications would give some indication of teaching effort. The OfS could play a helpful role in monitoring these data, commenting on trends, informing government policy and making information available in a useful form for the public without placing further burdens on institutions or requiring large expenditure in assessing submissions.

If the purpose of the TEF is to provide information for students and others, why not just provide potentially relevant data without seeking to aggregate in a way that is influenced by the essay submissions from senior administrators and that may not reflect the interests of a particular student. It is far better, we would argue, to present data in a clear way, and let the student interpret the information. If we were to give advice to a student, we would view the student–staff ratio (SSR) as the most useful measure. When outputs – education quality – are hard to measure, it is sometimes useful to measure inputs. If one department has an SSR of 30 students per staff member, and another an SSR of ten students per staff member in the same subject, there is a likelihood that lecturers are more accessible to students in the second department.

We are cognisant that the student is making a decision for the next three years that will influence their life, and one that is hard to reverse – transferring from one subject to another, much less from one university to another, is a difficult process. This decision needs, as in the past, to be guided by the information from institutions and by visits to the department where the student is considering a course. It is for the university to define and market its mission. The website should provide real information for students about what the programme is intending to achieve, but the student needs to go to the campus and see for themselves its tone and feel. Students are alert enough to know that the department has chosen the student guides and the sample lectures to attend, as well as those giving the open day presentations, and will use their own common sense in seeing behind the curtain and coming to a judgement on the best university for themselves.

The OIA

The need to focus on the student experience following the introduction of fees also saw the introduction of a limited ombudsman system, the Office of the Independent Adjudicator (OIA). We describe the history of its formation in the Short Note on setting up the OIA. We feel that much greater use could be made of the OIA and its ombudsman approach.

The purpose of the OIA is to provide an independent judgement on complaints from students that remained unresolved by the internal process. Its approach from the outset had as a major objective a general improvement in complaints handling procedures across the system and one of cooperation among institutions through shared workshops and publication of case studies. Institutions are not identified except for those which have refused to accept the recommendations, although extensive data is published. There is no attempt to rank institutions in league tables.

The spread of good practice is not confined to improvements in complaints procedures. For example, in looking at complaints about claimed unjust accusations of plagiarism it was apparent (even when the complaint was not upheld) that some students were generally unclear as to what constitutes plagiarism. Investigation of these issues enabled the OIA to share thoughts on how to clarify what can be a difficult area and to encourage the spread of constructive ideas.

Raising quality by lowering the SSR

We have observed the irony that the intention of introducing market forces into the university sector, and letting students as consumers drive the quality of education upwards, has ultimately led to greater and greater intervention when the markets didn't work. In earlier chapters, we argued that the markets were poorly designed and provided little incentive for universities to increase the quality of provision. The answer is not to have further bureaucratic oversight, such as with the TEF, but (if the market approach is to be retained) to re-design the markets and to restore traditional oversight in the form of the external examination system. We come back to this in our final chapter discussing future policy.

We have observed that, if we were allowed one metric for judging educational provision in a department or university, we would look at the SSR. This shows how many academics are available relative to the number of students. As noted above, when outputs (educational value) are hard to measure, it can sometimes be sensible to look at inputs. Small classes, reasonable numbers of students being assigned to each personal advisor, and controlled teaching and marking loads all benefit education. It is the SSR that determines the possibilities for this high-value style of teaching. The supply of administrators, particularly in academic departments, and other support and expenditures can assist, but at the end of the day it is the number of people at the coalface that is determinative of quality. Close and sympathetic attention to students also gives the sort of day-to-day support which is more likely to reduce the stress and anxiety that has been observed to be on the increase, or at the very least provide an opportunity to spot it early.

As student fees have increased there has been a significant increase in income. Figure 5.1 (which graphs expenditures year by year, as opposed to the snapshots in Figure 1.2) shows how the expenditure has been distributed across categories.

Figure 5.1 shows that, of recurrent expenditures, the growth has been fairly evenly spread across each budget (academic staff costs, administrative staff costs, other expenditure). The share spent on academic staff costs – the frontline workers – has gone down modestly. This is consistent with our discussion of stakeholder power in Chapter Four, with a weakening in the decision-making influence of academics in the university in favour of managers.

There has been an overall increase in spending of about 20 per cent. This has led to a welcome reduction on average of SSRs (see Figure 5.2).

Figure 5.1: Expenditures across categories

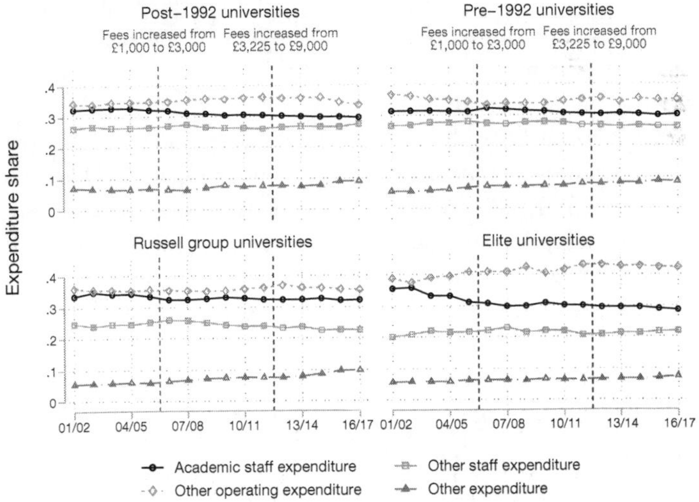

Note: HE institutions with fewer than ten students are excluded in this figure.

Source: HESA Finance Record 2001/02–2016/17

Figure 5.2: Student to staff ratio (SSR)

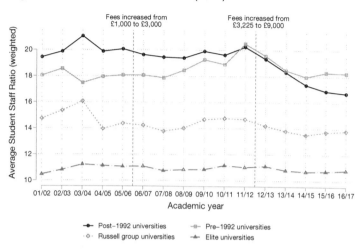

Note: HE institutions with fewer than ten students are excluded in this figure. The institutions' total student numbers are used for weighting.

Source: HESA Student and Staff Record 2001/02–2016/17

However, for all but the post-1992 universities, this has only taken us back to the levels seen in 2007/08, consequent then upon the fee level rising from £1000 to £3000. Further, the larger improvement at the post-1992 universities has more to do with a fall in student numbers (Figure 3.1) than with a conscious decision to improve the academic environment.

What could have been done can be illustrated by looking at the increase in income at universities. Income per HEU (home and non-UK European Union) student has gone up by 50 per cent following the increase in fees. If the SSRs had adjusted in proportion, they would have dropped by 1/3. While this is an overstatement, since the other income sources for universities (overseas student fees, research income, and so on) did not rise in proportion, it is the calculation that a home student might reasonably make in asking whether or not they were receiving value for money for their tripled fees.

Is the current situation sustainable?

When one looks at the difference between total income and total recurrent expenditure one might ask where the difference has gone. As anyone visiting (and students recently attending) an English university knows, the differential has been reflected in the turning of university campuses into building sites. High quality buildings have always been important for creating a good environment for teaching and research and more of this space will be necessary if ambitions for expansion are realised. Improvements to existing stock are also to be welcomed. But some of the explosion in building projects has been aimed at attracting more students rather than improving the educational environment. Sports centres, gyms, shopping malls, student unions may improve the general life for students but their contribution to academic excellence is not so convincing. There is as well an equity consideration since much of the expenditure is arising from the surplus accruing from increased fees paid by current students. To that extent, it is being funded by current students for the benefit of future cohorts. Current students instead just suffer the inconveniences of being on a building site and face a long-term student loan debt to pay for it. This seems to us a strong argument for why students who paid £9000 a year in the last few years should equitably have some of those funds returned as credits to their student loan accounts in the event that fees are lowered for future students.

Funding for the building projects has come from a variety of sources: a recent build-up of cash from annual surpluses, previous accrued reserves, long-term borrowing and some relatively small capital grants. Even if borrowing locks in current low interest rates with long-term loans, new buildings require ongoing maintenance and staffing. Universities seem to be relying on increasing student numbers and current fee levels to meet these future costs. On the basis of projections of population growth, there is some reason to be sanguine that the number of potential students will be sufficient to fill university places, if a 50 per cent participation rate remains the goal. Even then, it is unlikely that fees will be maintained at current real levels, and they may well be cut to appease both students and the taxpayer. Further, contributions to the pension scheme will need to rise and the public sector pay cap is being relaxed.

In the medium term, high student debt may limit the number of students going on for advanced degrees and becoming the lecturers of the future, particularly given the increasing casualisation of the academic workforce.

Universities seem to be assuming that they will all thrive and stake their plans on the basis of little change in the current environment. However, the government has made clear its intention to expand private provision, which will recruit students at the expense of the existing institutions. As we discuss in Chapter Six, in the Short Note on the case for career colleges, based upon the US experience, this is likely to be a mistake and lower quality if the private provision extends to traditional degree subjects and not externally-certified vocational subjects. However, we do feel that there should be increasing recognition of the importance of the FE and non-degree HE sectors as alternative educational routes. These provide a crucial service to local communities and businesses and have traditionally provided opportunities for school leavers to learn new skills as well as to adults wanting to retrain, update skills or seek cultural enrichment. Further, these alternatives have provided a lower-cost programme enabling students to follow foundation pathways towards university. Ironically, under the 2011 funding changes, the taxpayer is supporting universities charging £9000 a year offering newly-integrated foundation years as part of a four-year undergraduate degree, rather than these lower-cost alternatives.

Even leaving aside lower-cost alternatives, potential students may simply decide that the financial investment required under the current funding scheme does not make sense for them. While we think that this is too 'transactional' a view of university education, students are currently being told to think predominantly in terms of the employability aspects of their degree. The value of a degree then derives from the 'graduate premium' – graduates earn more. Any data on this is necessarily retrospective, but as the number of graduates increases clearly the premium will be reduced. Recent data[1] shows that six months after graduation almost half of employed new graduates are in non-graduate jobs and even after three years, 25 per cent remain so. Interestingly those graduating in STEM subjects perform among the worst. This supports the view, contrary to government pronouncements, that employers value the 'soft' skills developed in the humanities and social sciences and that the value of a university education derives from coming to grips with difficult ideas, stretching the mind, knowing how to frame a question and to communicate your views, irrespective of the particular course studied.

The STEM subjects are important in that there needs to be a general improvement in basic numeracy and scientific method and understanding if citizens are to play a part in society. And there is an equally important but much more limited need for mathematical and scientific graduates at the highest level to fuel future research and provide for the next generation of teachers at schools and universities. It will be up to well qualified teachers if we are to improve general scientific literacy. Secondary teachers in mathematics, physics and chemistry (along with engineers, physical scientists and IT specialists) are on the Shortage Occupation List for Tier 2 visas, showing that more still needs to be done in these specific areas.

The employment payoff to STEM subjects, however, is not as strong in the aggregate as employers seek more generic skills. Questions should be asked about the kneejerk reliance of universities on how the new technologies will support demand for places in the STEM subjects. It is important not to conflate all STEM subjects together, or to assume that demand for the growth in technology will not also lead to a greater demand for humanities backgrounds. Some teaching grant (both the currently remaining amount and potential new direct funding to universities in return for lower fees) might optimally be spent on leaning against the wind and supporting subjects in areas under pressure because of a current falloff in student demand. Once humanities subjects are lost it is very difficult for them to be reinstated. The challenges of the new technologies will require technical skills to compete but also an ability to ask hard questions and address ethical issues and an understanding of how these perennial questions have occupied previous generations and civilisations. The current instrumental approach to education seems to disregard the quality of life fostered by the Arts and Humanities. The problem starts at school level where changes in the curriculum have downgraded the humanities and creative arts in favour of the more measurable skills in the STEM subjects. And even in the humanities we have seen the introduction of highly restrictive syllabuses and focused assessments stunting creativity and experimentation. This is unlikely to make the pursuit of these subjects at university more attractive. As a consequence, universities with demanding courses in the humanities have trouble recruiting students, because interest and skills in these areas have not been nurtured in schools to the extent they once were. If this leads to difficulties in maintaining these departments at universities, not only will employers suffer the shortage but so will school teaching and the downward spiral will continue.

There are therefore considerable risks for universities, even leaving aside shifting political winds. There is acute concern in all parties about the current level of debt incurred by students which the threshold on earnings before repayment through a tax surcharge does little to offset. Do students really feel that three years' hard work and a £50,000 debt is worth it for a salary modestly above the repayment threshold income, particularly if authorities are regularly trying to convince them to judge the merit of a degree by its 'employability'? How does the threshold support the notion of helping the disadvantaged into university when the policy does nothing to reduce the financial commitment, only to help out if it doesn't turn out well? And even for those who do find a good and secure career many will be paying what is in effect a graduate tax surcharge of 9 per cent and still leaving an unpaid debt at the end of the write-off period of 30 years. For example, a teacher progressing through an 'average earnings' career under the old regime of £3000 fees would repay around £25,000, paying off the full loan by the age of 40. Under the new regime repayments would continue until the age of 50 and amount to about £42,000 and still leave a debt of £25,000 to be written off.

Written-off debt, while an intentional part of the system as the way of achieving redistribution and insurance, is not without consequence.[3] The total debt to be written off was forecast by the Office for Budget Responsibility (OBR) in 2011 to be £50 billion by 2030 assuming average tuition fees of £7,500 rising by inflation.[4] The accounting devices employed by the government, including selling off the debt at disadvantageous rates for the taxpayer has been analysed by the Head of the Institute of Fiscal Studies[5] and more recently criticised by the Public Accounts Committee. We are not convinced that current funding to universities – incorporated not only in the high level of student fees but also in maintenance loans contributing to high accommodation costs – will or should be continued into the future. In a period of austerity, government debt taken on today to make advance payments to universities (in the up-front fees of £9000) will have to be repaid by the very generation of students who are supposedly benefiting from the taxpayer support. In a very real sense, those students who earn enough to repay their student loans (and therefore won't be receiving any subsidy) will also be repaying the debt of others, and those who do not repay their loans will still find themselves, as general members of society, suffering the fiscal effects of government debt. Future governments inheriting this debt will either need to increase revenues or cut expenditures.

Impact on new academics

There has been increasing realisation by university managements of these uncertainties and caution has manifested itself in a transference of both risk and financial stringency (perhaps even to the point of poverty) to new entrants to the profession with increasing casualisation, and to established academics through proposals to decimate pension commitments. Managers may also in the future seek redundancies in restructuring away from currently unfashionable subjects to adding more and more degrees and student places in currently popular areas, not realising that this will create an oversupply in those areas that will eventually cause a collapse in the market and leave them unprepared as, in all probability, the unfashionable returns to popularity.

The best university managements, guided by listening to their senior academics, will not follow down the road of these short-term measures. Maintaining the quality of the product through thick and thin is the way to survive and prosper in any economic environment. With respect to maintaining excellence in out-of-fashion subjects, it is simply the case that hard-nosed practicality for a management willing to hold its nerve will realise that if others retreat from the game they will still be able to fish in an albeit depleted pool. It is the copycat universities that will struggle when competition is restored to the higher education market. But every university depends upon the system as a whole producing good PhDs who are attracted to the academic market, and are given the support and opportunity to develop their research and teaching skills. Universities cannot and should not run the risk of inbreeding by seeking to be self-sufficient if the sector as a whole is under-performing.

It has always been the case that permanent academic jobs take a long to time to find, depending upon the field of study; doctoral, postdoctoral and probationary periods have been a featured rite of passage. But the disturbing advance of a 'gig-economy' is a vicious twist to this tale. This not only puts a severe strain on aspiring academics in terms of day-to-day security but disables their opportunities for research and general career development needed to enhance their prospects for secure employment. Further, there has been a trend towards reducing the rate of pay for casual teaching. Visiting lecturers, on an hourly paid basis, were traditionally paid for two hours of preparation and marking, for each hour of classroom teaching. This is now being reduced, effectively lowering pay for the least well-paid members of the teaching staff. This is not only a human disgrace but has an effect on the student experience not considered by central auditors more interested in institutional process and a hunt for measurable data than the value of young academics on whom the future standing of our universities depends.

This austerity for academic staff, in a context of general liquidity in budgets, has extended to pensions and created the recent (ongoing) pensions dispute. Setting aside questions of policy about estimating shortfalls in pension schemes in general, provisions for pensions enter into university balance sheets and it may be for that reason that the employers' body, the UUK (Universities UK), was so adamant on reducing pension commitments (see Figure 5.3).

In summary, present policy presents a risk to public finances, a probable disillusion for those students from disadvantaged backgrounds whom it purports to help and a risk to the future standing of our universities. While purporting to make all universities more equal, it has had the opposite effect and solidified the natural research hierarchy that holds in academic life. Most profoundly, the focus on the balance sheet has removed the fundamental value and excitement of academic life for new PhDs entering the profession and for their students.

Figure 5.3: Pension liabilities appearing on university balance sheets

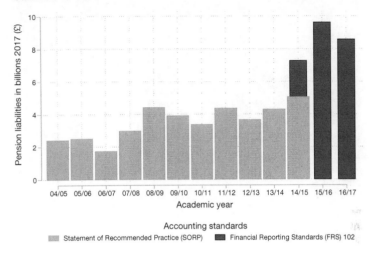

Note: HE institutions with fewer than ten students are excluded in this figure.

Source: HESA Finance Record 2004/05–2016/17

A Short Note On: Setting up the OIA

When the new fees system was introduced following the Dearing Report it was anticipated that the number of student complaints might increase. At the time, pre-1992 universities had various internal procedures for dealing with complaints. Under the 'visitorial system' unresolved complaints were referred to an independent 'visitor'. In some university statutes, this role resided in a particular office (for several it was the Monarch), for others an independent person of standing was appointed by the university. The visitor's task was to adjudicate on complaints by staff and students against the university's obligations under its Charter – the original concern being from founders who wanted to ensure their founding intentions were being maintained. The polytechnics had a variety of arrangements, many had none.

The Committee of Vice-Chancellors and Principals (CVCP) launched an investigation and asked for recommendations on the way forward. Having determined proposals it launched a consultation exercise in 2000. These met with considerable opposition, ranging from 'What's the problem?' to 'We don't want a one size fits all' and 'It's been fine for 500 years why change?' The idea of an 'ombudsman' was anathema to many. To be fair this was at a time of unease over creeping government control and this was seen by some in that context. However, it was also a time of a general tendency in the population to be more litigious and large legal bills looked a distinct possibility. It was also argued in the consultation that there was much to be gained from universities learning good practice from each other in their handling of complaints. Just as students should expect some baseline level for academic standards, why should they not expect some consistency in the manner in which complaints were handled. The CVCP was replaced by UUK but the work continued under their auspices.

A second round of consultation avoided the term 'ombudsman' in favour of 'The Office of the Independent Adjudicator for Student Complaints' (OIA) and provided more detail as to how such an office would work, how it would be funded and how it would maintain independence. It also emphasised how it would identify and disseminate good practice. This second round received a high level of support. Government expressed a wish to establish something along these lines in an upcoming Act and asked UUK to develop the ideas. UUK set up a small steering group and working with civil servants proceeded on drafting the relevant section of the Higher Education Act 2004.

When the Act was passed, UUK was given a budget to recruit the first staff, find and set up an office and get the thing on the road. One of the authors (NG) was appointed Chair, the first Independent Auditor, Baroness Ruth Deech, was appointed and the OIA was set up in 2004 with an office in Reading. Because of budget restrictions the office space would have to be smaller than eventually would be required and staff appointed more slowly than needed until subscriptions came in. Case handlers were largely people with legal experience. The work of the Office was overseen by a Board. The membership of the Board was (and still is) made up of nominations from sector bodies including UUK, NUS, and GuildHE as well as independent members who were in the majority. Several of these independent members had valuable experience of other ombudsman schemes. Although those from the sector were nominated they were not serving as representatives. The intention was to bring relevant experience of working in the sector, not to act as lobbyists for the various bodies by whom they had been nominated. There was considerable political opposition to the appointment of both the first Chair of the Board and the first Independent Adjudicator coming from the university sector (Ruth Deech was a legal academic and former Principal of St Anne's Oxford but had the credentials of having chaired the Human Fertilisation and Embryo Authority). But it was argued that winning the support of the sector was still fragile and would best be maintained, at least in the initial phase, by seeing the office steered by people who knew something about the issues. After a few years,

Ruth moved on and was replaced by someone from outside the sector and after two terms the Chair was succeeded by someone from outside the university world. Once some confidence from the sector had been established and the fuss about the term ombudsman forgotten, the OIA joined the Ombudsman Association which helped staff develop their own professional expertise and keep up to date with best practice.

Funding is by subscription varying by size of institution. Funding by subscription was laid down in legislation and made compulsory. This device helped maintain independence of the office. It was not reliant on government funding and not reliant on keeping institutions happy. (Later, subscriptions were augmented by a case fee to encourage good internal procedures and fewer cases. Cases were – and are – brought by students at no cost to them.) The scheme receives complaints only after internal procedures have been completed. (One of the early introductions was the issue of recommended forms for letters of completion of procedure when it was suspected that some universities were being less than clear, making it difficult for students to know whether they were yet eligible to lodge a complaint.) The Office would not receive complaints about admission procedures or ones against academic judgement. So, for example, a complaint can be brought if it is claimed that an examination board had not been properly constituted or had not followed proper procedures, but not against the judgement of a properly conducted board. Subscriptions were set (and remain) well below potential legal costs which might otherwise ensue. It remains open to a student who remains dissatisfied with the judgement to appeal for judicial review. Several of these have been requested, most have been refused by the judiciary, of those that have gone to review very few have been against the OIA. (Data is available on the OIA website.)

The OIA continues to run workshops on good practice which are welcomed by universities because in the end, apart from the issue of fairness, good systems save costs. Cases found in favour of the student can result in a number of recommendations (the OIA has no power of compulsion – an important issue in the consultation process): compensation to the student (for example, free repeat of the course, or financial compensation, based on a judgement of actual financial loss, course fees or other costs) to be paid by the institution, recommendations for improvement of process (even when finding in favour of the university). From the outset emphasis was put on the collection and propagation of good data. Although its recommendations are not binding, those institutions not accepting the recommendations are named.

Although the number of complaints has increased steadily it is difficult to disaggregate from overall growth of students, the uneven numbers from different subject areas and categories of students and the increasing variety of institutions the OIA is now responsible for. The raw data is all there, however, and one can drill down to institutional level.

There was some talk of the OIA being rolled up into the new OfS, but in the end it remained free standing, but since its data is freely available it can be used to inform the OfS. The recent Education Act widened the responsibilities of the OIA to cover any institution approved and registered with OfS.

6

Widening Participation and Student Finance

There exists a large untapped potential among the less advantaged members of society. There is a moral responsibility towards these citizens and a social and economic reward for society as a whole if they could be provided with opportunities similar to those more fortunate by the circumstances of their birth. The surest way to address this problem is to tackle it as early as possible. The 1944 Education Act (passed by a Tory Secretary of State) had as its stated principle that 'The nature of a child's education should be based on (their) capacity and promise and not by the circumstances of (the) parent.' Recent attacks on early years' provision and the Sure Start programme, the emphasis on rote learning and testing in schools and the marginalisation of the humanities and creative arts, especially in state schools have been a backward step as has the loss of status of teachers in the mind of government. The first priority must be to address this failure, but that lies beyond the scope of this book. However, it is a good part of the reason that we have imposed the discipline upon ourselves to propose policies that do not involve any further public expenditure on higher education. The funds are simply needed more in the primary and secondary levels of education.

It is an important part of stated government policy to widen participation in universities, and in particular throughout the entire sector including the most elite universities. Government policy, incorporated in and developing upon the Browne Report, laid emphasis on the enhanced earning potential of graduates who should therefore bear some of the costs, ameliorated by policies around actual earnings of graduates. This reflected thinking that the prime purpose of education is personal financial gain and where this did not transpire, either by career choice or lack of graduate jobs, some help would be available through non-payback of loan. The fact that a significant amount of the loans would not be paid back was regarded as an acceptable recognition that society benefits as well as the graduate.

Research by London Economics for the Sutton Trust[1] has revealed rich data on participation rates. The pattern for the decade up to 2016 showed that while participation increased over the whole range of household incomes, the special benefit to those from low income backgrounds was modest. In 2006, 8 per cent of the most disadvantaged post-18 cohort went to university compared with 47 per cent of the most advantaged, a gap of 39 percentage points. In 2016, these figures were respectively 14 per cent and 52 per cent, a gap of 38 percentage points. Furthermore, a higher proportion of the increase from low income households has gone to low tariff universities (4 per cent of the low income post-18 cohort went to university at these institutions in 2006 rising to 7 per cent in 2016) compared with those going to high tariff universities (1.4 per cent to 2.3 per cent). The gap in participation rates from high and low income households at high tariff universities has remained stubbornly constant at 22 per cent between 2006 and 2016. The elimination of maintenance grants in favour of loans from 2016 is likely to exacerbate the situation.

There can be little doubt that the prospect of facing large debts on graduation is more off-putting to those from families with little financial security and, further, students from lower income backgrounds will receive less parental support and therefore will end up with higher loans. Valuable insight is again afforded by the Sutton Trust report.[1] This looks at government reaction in late 2017 to increasing concern about current policy: it froze fee levels at the current level and increased the threshold at which repayments start in an attempt to address growing debt to students. The research demonstrates that this revision saves graduates £8000 on average over their lifetime (in real terms) but increases long-term costs to the public purse through unpaid debt by £2.9 billion and an increase of unpaid loan from 27.6 per cent to 45.1 per cent: a problem for some future government. Average debts at graduation will be £46,000, with graduates from the bottom 40 per cent of households owing on average £51,600 compared to an average of £38,400 for those from the highest 20 per cent household earnings. Fully 81 per cent of students will never pay back their loans, compared to 76 per cent at present.

The contingent-repayment loan scheme

We view the current scheme as economically inefficient since it rewards failure, with the bulk of the subsidy directed towards poor outcomes from poorly-designed programmes. It is only directed specifically towards widening participation insofar as it is assumed that students from lower-income backgrounds will do relatively badly in their post-degree careers, or that those students are particularly risk-averse. We think both of those assumptions are socially divisive. Remarkably, the high interest rates on student loans mean that – as shown by Johnston[2] – the system is actually regressive over much of the middle range of incomes.

Johnston uses the online government calculators to show the regressive effect. We do this in a model that helps us explore how the scheme compares to a standard graduate tax and how the regressive effect arises when interest rates are high. Figure 6.1 shows the total repayment on a loan of roughly £50,000 on the assumption that the real income of the individual is constant over their career and that – contrary to the current system – the real interest rate is zero. That is, the remaining unpaid student debt goes up by the rate of inflation each year. We compare this to a graduate tax at a fixed rate. The income-contingent loan scheme differs by having a high marginal repayment rate on middle incomes, with no repayment on low incomes and a zero-marginal repayment rate on high incomes. Having the middle incomes bear the burden in this way makes little sense to us. It rewards failure in the terms of the policy measure of financial success by targeting the subsidy to those with career earnings averaging less than £25,000. It is hard to see why, in general, students should be encouraged to go to university on particular courses where there is an outcome of significant likelihood of ending up in a non-graduate job. Even if the policymaker thought that individuals on lower *ex post* incomes should receive the bulk of the subsidy in this way, a better alternative in our view is a fixed surcharge on the individual's income tax bill. This would then raise nothing from those individuals whose incomes were so low that they weren't paying tax, but would subsequently be progressive and in particular raise the greatest income from higher-rate taxpayers.

Figure 6.1: Zero real interest rate repayment graph

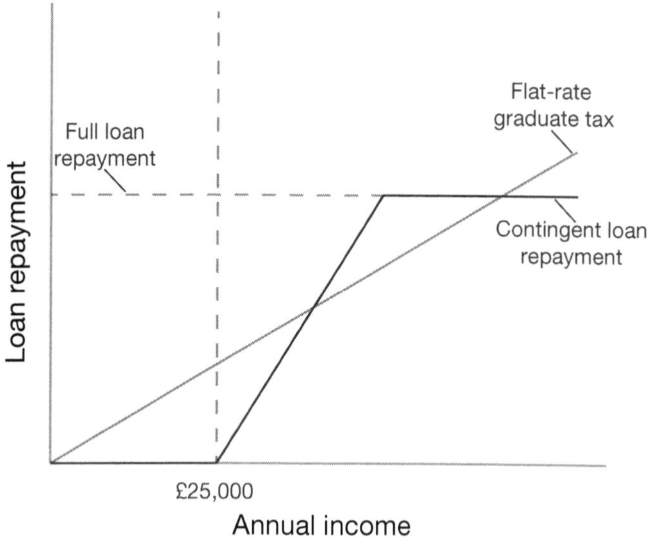

When the real interest rate charged is positive then the current scheme is actually regressive in the middle range. This is seen in Figure 6.2. Very successful graduates (and particularly those who gain funding from their parents and therefore borrowed less in the first place) repay the loans quickly, incurring little in interest payments. In contrast, those in the middle pay off the loans more slowly, and therefore incur significant interest payments. The current rate of interest is RPI (Retail Price Index) + 3 per cent while studying and for those with incomes over £45,000, with a sliding scale in between. This is punitive, partially in that it uses the RPI which typically shows a higher inflation rate than the CPI (Consumer Price Index) used for other government purposes. But it is also well in excess of the cost of funds to the government. The average 30-year gilt (government bond) yields 1.77 per cent at the moment. This includes inflation plus a negative real return. The government would therefore break even (except for the rate of non-payment which would be much lower than under the present scheme) at an interest rate of 1.77 per cent.

Figure 6.2: Positive real interest rate repayment graph

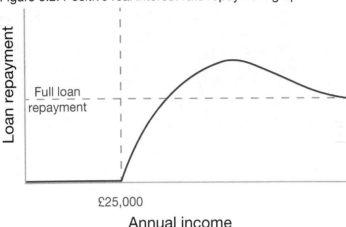

£25,000

Annual income

While students who do reasonably well are actually profitable for the government, repaying more than the government-financed student loans by the difference between the charged interest rate and the rate the government pays on its borrowing, it can be argued that students nonetheless benefit from having access to this finance. The private sector may not provide loans against education due to a market failure. The private sector might view loans to students as risky, particularly if – as is encouraged by the current student loans scheme – students can use the loans to take poorly-designed and delivered courses. A way around that, used in North America in some cases, is for the university to offer the loan. This then gives the university the right incentive to admit students who can benefit from the programme and will be in a position to repay the loans. Given the low endowments of most English universities, that is not a practical option (although we have argued that alumni donations can over time build up substantial pools of funds for scholarships or loans). When the government takes on this responsibility, as in England, it needs to take on a major role in quality assurance, as discussed in the preceding chapter. Simply, the government will gain a greater rate of repayment on student loans with greater quality control.

Up-front subsidies

The current loan scheme suffers from both a 'moral hazard' problem and an 'adverse selection' problem. 'Moral hazard' in economics is when an individual or firm has an incentive to behave badly – in this case, the individual might choose a course with low academic standards to have a fun three years, and the university might offer such courses to make the surplus on fees over costs. 'Adverse selection' is when individuals of unprofitable types crowd into a market due to the offer in the market, and potentially cause the market to collapse. A standard example is health insurance. People with poor health buy insurance, while young people in good health self-insure. As a consequence, prices for private health insurance rise, exacerbating the effect. Consider an 18-year-old who is considering becoming an accountant. If they go to university, they are likely to repay their student loans in full and – because of the punitive interest rate and the high £9000 fees – end up paying well above the costs of their education. Instead, they can train directly with a firm, take examinations from the professional bodies and get marketable qualifications and avoid going to university entirely, getting help in their studies through FE and other routes.

These are economic efficiency arguments against the loan scheme as currently structured. We also feel, however, that it is socially divisive in its assumption – if the aim is to widen participation – that students from lower income groups, often with qualifications that do not reflect their true potential, will typically end up with low incomes after university. This tends to lead to self-reinforcing stereotypes. The rest of the system, however, as we describe below, also tends to shunt such students into the lower-tariff universities, and often weaker programmes, again reinforcing the perception that these students by virtue of the circumstances of their birth have lower potential. Further, the proportion of subsidy directed at widening participation is limited by the poor targeting of the subsidy based on *ex post* incomes rather than *ex ante* need for support. As we have said, the system subsidises failure and therefore – by basic economics – you will get a lot of it. Instead, we want all students and all universities to aim high and, to the maximum extent supportable by the system, achieve those ambitions.

Directing the benefits of subsidy towards the less well-off necessarily involves some combination of means testing of fees and restoring maintenance grants. A possible model has been developed by London Economics for the Sutton Trust.[1] The London Economics analysis is based on a system assuming means-tested fees: those from household incomes of less than £25,000 pay nothing, increasing by steps of £3000–£3250 in fees for every increase of £25,000 in income up to a fee of £12,250 for incomes above £100,000. The model suggests that this shift to means-tested fees could cut the average student debt by a half, with the debt to the least well-off reduced from £51,600 to £12,700 compared to the best-off with debts of £38,400. Against this would be the potential costs of increasing the teaching grant to make up for the average fall in fees (since only students from well-off backgrounds would pay the current £9250 or the higher £12,250). The extra costs to the public purse would be partially offset by a higher proportion of student loans being repaid, with the percentage of graduates who never pay back their loans falling from 81 per cent to 65 per cent, so the net cost would be £2.5 billion per cohort. If maintenance grants were also reintroduced, the total cost would be £3.2 billion for each cohort. The Sutton Trust estimates that eliminating fees entirely would cost £4.6 billion per cohort.

Various models can be developed and the Sutton Trust proposal is but one example. It is not one we would particularly endorse since we are not convinced that even students from well-off backgrounds should pay £12,250, if the true cost of their education is at the Browne level of £6,000. A university education has a significant public good component, and we do not want anyone discouraged from going to university. However, following through on this particular model and assuming that the lost fee income from means testing is to be made up by an increase in the teaching grant (as it might have to because to do otherwise would make disadvantaged students less attractive financially) there would be an upfront cost to the taxpayer. However, long-term debt would be reduced and it is only the 'weird and wonderful world of government accounting for student loans' that obscures a net potentially positive calculation.[3]

There can be little doubt that the prospect of facing large debts on graduation is more off-putting to those from families with little financial security. We therefore think that a return to means-tested fee and maintenance support is one important plank in widening participation. A given amount of government subsidy is more effectively targeted on low income households. But the extremely low rates of university participation – particularly at high tariff universities – of disadvantaged students is unlikely to be addressed exclusively by a return to low fees and maintenance payments. We are cognisant that the low participation rate preceded the imposition of high fees.

The current system: access agreements with the Office for Fair Access

Removing the subsidy to failure in the current funding scheme is one plank in our approach, the use of means testing to direct subsidies to those from less advantaged backgrounds is another, but we still need to get high tariff and other universities to target admissions to ensure fair access.

We take Oxford and Cambridge admissions tutors at their word – and since these decisions are made by College Fellows whose motivations we observe on a regular basis to be generally progressive – that they make efforts to recruit more state school pupils and those from less advantaged backgrounds. At present, there is considerable moral pressure exerted on universities to improve participation and universities are required by the Office for Fair Access (OFFA) to have plans for improving access if they are to be allowed to charge the maximum fee. It is not clear just how this will be continued by the Office for Students (OfS), but it is recognised by the government that to date there has been only modest improvement in access to high tariff universities.

There are disincentives to university staff. Even the talented student from an impoverished background is likely to be less well prepared for the change of study environment or technically in terms of essay writing or, say, mathematical techniques than one of similar innate talents who has benefited from an expensive education and an intellectually rich home environment. The disadvantaged students are therefore likely to need more help in the early stage of their university careers and university staff may not have the same skills to provide this as schoolteachers, and in any case, it is an extra call on their time when this has of recent years come under increasing pressure. Arguably, however, these issues are more severe with overseas students, particularly from non-English speaking countries. Because of the uncapped numbers and fees for overseas students, universities have nonetheless greatly expanded intake of these students. This has not held with home and European Union students from underrepresented groups, as there is no *per student* extra financial incentive to widen participation.

In order to charge the higher fee level of £9000, the university must have an access agreement with at least one defined target, but – from the OFFA website – 'we would not apply a sanction solely on the basis of you not meeting your targets or milestones'. To have a concrete example, we take the 2018–19 University of Bristol access agreement with OFFA. This observes that the university gains £46.9 million from charging the higher fee compared to the 'basic' £6000 and commits that 'In 2018–19 the University of Bristol will invest 30.7 per cent of its additional fee income in additional access measures to include: financial support for students from low income backgrounds and a comprehensive programme of activities to support outreach, retention, and progression of students from underrepresented groups.' The expenditures are on outreach activities (£3.4 million), student success and progression activities (£1.9 million), and student finance (£9.1 million).

The agreement goes on at great length (38 pages) to discuss in detail all the programmes undertaken by the university for outreach, again an example of how the current university funding system maximises the essay writing of senior administrators. It is hard to understand why the OFFA needs to know about the detailed programmes undertaken by the university, although the information is no doubt of considerable value for internal planning and could be shared between universities to develop best practice across comparable institutions and the sector. But, in our view, this is precisely the sort of micro-management and form filling that is not a desirable function of the regulator. The regulator should determine the targets for access and leave it to the university to find the best ways of meeting those targets. As it stands at the moment universities offer targets and process but are 'not necessarily' sanctioned if targets are not achieved.

After all the discussion in the agreement, the bottom line is that the maximum bursary at Bristol – to a student with a family residual household income under £25,000 – is £2000. We find it hard to understand how this is of an even approximately right magnitude for a serious effort at recruiting students from under-represented groups. And it may be observed that these bursaries and the cost of outreach programmes (direct, administrative and opportunity costs) is met by the fellow students who are paying full fees.

Applications and admissions

It must be up to the university – particularly high-tariff universities – actively to recruit good students from under-represented groups. In keeping with our approach of encouraging excellence, we would want the system to ensure that students from these groups attain equal achievement to other, privileged, groups within the university. As with university competition in general, we don't want universities, for example, to admit BME students by taking them from the next tier in the hierarchy and not providing any support needed to overcome weaker school preparation, lack of extra tutoring and other benefits gained by students from privileged backgrounds.

Having said that, a student with A level grades of ABB from a school which has not in the past sent a student to a high ranked university probably shows more ability and potential than one achieving a similar result after 13 years at a costly independent school and highly supportive parenting. Indeed, there is evidence that students from less privileged backgrounds perform better at the end of their university career than those with the same entry grades from selective schools. It is hardly surprising; they have to be exceptionally talented to get there in the first place. But the current process of application does not assist. It is difficult for admissions tutors to make judgements given the current information available. They know the name of the school, the predicted A level grades, previous exam performance and the written statement. Decisions have traditionally been taken before A level results are known and the reliability of these predictions has always been problematic. There is a natural tendency to keep taking students from the same schools where the admissions tutor knows how to interpret the predictions and the general high standard of the school. The recent news of a dramatic increase in unconditional offers is likely to reinforce this bias: universities that can pick and choose will take risks only from schools they feel they can trust.

These predictions on A-level results (and consequently the restricted potential for a high performing student from a less known school being admitted to a top university) will be even less reliable with the abolishment of AS levels.[4, 5] It is quite remarkable that in the face of protests about over-testing in schools the government has been resolute, yet in the face of advice about the value of AS levels they have been abolished. The evidence that AS levels have been useful supports the intuitive observation that the school attended together with GCSE results and AS results and predicted A levels gives a sense of forward momentum from perhaps a difficult start and can show promise of more to come.

Another piece of information available to the admissions tutor is the personal statement. Schools with a long tradition of preparing students for university are skilled at helping students write these statements, having experience of both the type of content that goes down well and the means of expression that finds favour with the university academic. Writing style has been honed through the school career to that common to academic discourse. Such experience is not so readily available in schools, especially in deprived areas where a disproportionate amount of time has to be spent on pupils who are really struggling, not found in selective schools.

Similarly, the advantaged student will likely have a much richer hinterland to provide opportunities to list extra-curricular activities which resonate well with those trying to select from oversubscribed courses. Advantages of birth are nourished and brought to fruition at the point of university application. These advantages are even stronger if applicants are faced with interviews for which they have been well rehearsed. Further, the whole process of the interview-intensive admissions at the top universities – combined with a feeling that 'I might not fit in' – conspires to make it challenging for the top universities to recruit students from non-traditional sources and under-represented groups.

There is an argument for central, national admissions processes as are used in some contexts for assigning new doctors to hospitals and in some countries, university lecturers to universities. Once students are assigned a priority for admission, it would be up to the individual universities to compete to recruit the best students from the pool. Indeed, the Browne report required some sort of mechanism to determine which students would be eligible for loans under the capped overall numbers in the system. While Browne seems to have undue confidence in being able to determine a common tariff on the basis of A-level results (although he does recognise that non-standard qualifications need a separate system), some sort of central planning for deciding eligibility for student loans could be envisaged, at least in part.

In the meantime, however, ways must be found to help those left behind. Getting rid of written statements on application forms and restoring AS levels would go some way. Talented students might also be advised to wait a year and apply with known good A levels under their belts. This requires some form of support and funding for the 'gap' year and perhaps provision of foundation or taster courses. Restoration of means-tested maintenance grants would widen choice beyond living at home and going to local universities, a limitation not just on choice of university but on the opportunity to live and study in a different environment. And a scheme of state funded scholarships for talented students from state schools, together with either the abolishment of fees or means testing of current or modified arrangements and reviewing the interest charged on loans would no doubt help widen choice.

It cannot be emphasised strongly enough that although these comments are concerned with access to the high tariff universities they are in no way meant to downgrade other opportunities for higher education. High tariff universities want to attract students with high academic ability or potential and provide a challenging experience that suits them. This is no better nor worse than the opportunities provided by other parts of the system. The challenge is to provide diversity and access to whatever part of the system that best suits the individual and movement through the system for those who feel that they have made the wrong choice or who develop in unexpected ways. The present system of league tables ranks according to criteria dictated by a particular mission. Their present dominance is a pressure against diversity and an encouragement of the view that those going to the 'top' universities are better in every sense.

What works

Iris Bohnet,[6] in an important book on gender inequality, makes the point that one should just opportunistically focus upon policies that work. There is no fundamental infeasibility in achieving greater representation of disadvantaged groups throughout the higher education system. Oxford University could fill its places with highly qualified state school students in a way that matches the proportion in the overall pool of students, rather than having disproportionate numbers of those who have enjoyed a privileged private education. Its intake could readily match the diversity of the population of England. We see absolutely no reason why – as an institution in receipt of large amounts of state funding – it should fail to do so.

The question then becomes how best to achieve these targets, not just for Oxford, but for other universities where the recruitment issue may be more difficult. The mathematics – and the logic – of specific required targets are not generally understood. If Oxford were to be given a target on underrepresented groups such as BME, or state school, or proportions from different social classes, it would have many ways of achieving it. It can engage in active recruitment, it can set up foundation years, it can have bursaries (although these cannot be, for example, race related under UK law), it can offer free accommodation, and so on. Mathematically, Oxford would have a 'shadow price' related to admissions on the target group and this 'shadow price' is exactly like a penalty or reward set up by an agency such as the OFFA (if they did indeed choose to make targets effective). The adoption of means-tested fees and maintenance grants makes identification of less advantaged students an easy matter.

In early research, one of us (JF) studied the fuel economy standards required by the Environmental Protection Agency in the US. These were set at very stringent levels, with prohibitive penalties for any car manufacturer who failed to meet the targets, which were in the form of average fuel economy over the entire fleet of vehicles sold. A gainsayer might argue that this was unduly restrictive and would badly affect economic efficiency and might even bankrupt the auto companies. However, the companies were ingenious in responding to the standards by finding the most efficient way of meeting them. One method was – when the standard was particularly binding in a given year – to sell smaller cars at a loss to lower the average fuel usage over the fleet of cars and meet the standard, while simultaneously raising the price of large, fuel-inefficient cars. In the same way, we expect that Oxford could find a way of meeting student characteristic targets.

Setting specific targets works. There need be no discussion and no negotiation on a constant basis.

While – in our general approach to avoid micromanagement – we will favour specific targeted rewards or requirements for widening participation, there are potential pitfalls to avoid. An example arises from affordable housing in London that was originally set at a fixed percentage to apply to each new building project. Under that firm policy, the affordable housing percentage was necessarily met. Subsequently, developers were allowed to negotiate with local councils over alternatives to on-site affordable housing and – not surprisingly – the policy has been much less effective. A drawback of the targeted scheme however was that developers put in separate entrances ('poor doors') to the affordable housing part of their project and would use cheaper fittings and fixtures. More positively, perhaps, they would target the housing to teachers and nurses as desirable neighbours for those purchasing the expensive properties adjacent. We would not necessarily be disappointed if universities sought out the most 'worthy' students of less advantaged backgrounds, but would not wish these students to be subject to 'poor doors' or a lesser quality of education than their more privileged colleagues.

While targets represent one way forward, it has become more common to think of incentives in the form of subsidies or penalties such as fines. Indeed, there is a popular belief that 'positive reinforcement' in the form of subsidies works better than 'negative reinforcement' in the form of punishments. Interestingly,[7] research starting with Dickinson's paper in fact shows that 'penalties may be more effective than prizes'. We return to these issues in our final chapter on policy options.

Alternative providers

An important other way of thinking about widening participation is through non-traditional institutions. In the two Short Notes to this chapter, we consider the Open University (OU) in the UK and the role of private providers in the US.

Even a government that sets very rigorous targets for widening participation is unlikely to seek full equality of admissions and progression across ethnic and social groups in the immediate future. They could do so – it is as much a political as an economic decision how much and how fast to achieve equality of opportunity in the university system. In a context where preparation before age 18 differs widely across groups, declaring equality of entry at each university would realistically have implications for considerable costs to be incurred in bringing students of different levels of preparedness up to a reasonably common standard, or at least a standard where the student could realistically achieve a degree. But even then, how much do we try to address previous disparities through the traditional university sector? For current and future generations of 18-year-olds, during what will be an extended period before equality of opportunity is achieved, what can we offer those individuals who will not qualify for entry at traditional universities?

The OU was a very British solution to addressing higher education for those who had missed the traditional route into university at age 18. The OU has relied upon television and subsequently computers, along with traditional academic input in tutoring students and in summer schools. High academic standards were maintained for both students (with rigorous examinations with external examiners) and staff (with research being supported). Nonetheless, the nature of the provision is of lower cost than a traditional university, and the OU cannot be expected to achieve the same level of richness of experience and daily exposure to academics as for students in the higher cost full-time residential provision. What is important is that it is not just lower cost but is uniquely designed to be 'fit for purpose', as described in the Short Note on the Open University, below.

While the OU is a very British solution, private providers are a very American solution. The government has proposed the expansion of private providers in degree courses in a belief that these will represent an effective form of competition. Currently, as reported by HEFCE (Higher Education Funding Council for England), the bulk of private providers are small, are focused upon business and management studies, and are disproportionately (relative to traditional providers) attended by older and minority ethnic students. They are filling a gap, but one where the 'customer' might be viewed as most susceptible to miss-selling. The American experience, described in the Short Note below, is that these sorts of career colleges need particular oversight by the authorities and can succeed only where there are independent professional examinations that provide a concrete test of success of the programme.

This is in keeping with our overall view of the best way forward for the sector. Each institution should be excellent at what it does, but institutions should not all try to occupy the same market sphere. The traditional universities will be high cost due to the expense of providing a low student–staff ratio with teaching by leading researchers in the field. Other universities, particularly the post-1992 institutions, can focus upon teaching, run at a lower cost but still with an outstanding quality of education, and selected areas for research. For mature students who have greater motivation, the OU can provide a lower cost route to a good university degree. Sufficiently regulated and monitored private providers can – based upon the US experience – fulfil direct career and employability criteria at a relatively contained cost.

Where, in our view, the government makes a potential mistake is in conflating 'value for money' with 'low cost price competition'. Encouraging private providers to enter the market at a lower price point, for traditional degree subjects, is unlikely to increase quality competition and therefore 'value for money' at traditional universities. Further, private providers should be judged upon 'employability' since that is what – following the US model – their raison d'être should be as career colleges. Imposing that criterion as a primary measure of success for traditional universities and degrees, however, fails to understand what universities are established to accomplish.

A Short Note On: The Open University

The OU was a truly innovative addition to the Higher Education scene so it may be worth recalling its place in the system as conceived at its inception. Granted a Royal Charter in 1969 its purpose was to provide an opportunity for degree level study for adults working at home who had missed out on a university education, or wanted to update qualifications, change track or simply study for no other purpose than self-enrichment. Course material was prepared by a central core of full-time academics (sometimes with contributions by specialist consultants where necessary), comprising written material, television and radio programmes and, for science, home experimental kits, shipped to students' homes. Part-time staff drawn from other universities and polytechnics provided regular tutorials in study centres around the country and marked assignments, with marking schemes provided by the central course teams. These staff and the study centres were supported by regional centres staffed by academics from each faculty taking responsibility for the service to students in their region and also contributing to the central course teams. A course would typically comprise 32 course units to cover a 32-week teaching year. Some courses were supported also by week-long summer schools hosted at universities around the country. Once a course was written it would run for a few years (depending on the various different needs for keeping it up to date and refreshed) during which a smaller core group would set fresh assignments and examinations. Students had to pass eight courses to obtain an honours degree. Each course was intended to equate to a half a year's study at a conventional university, so the full programme represented four year's study, in recognition that there were no entry requirements. Each faculty offered a foundation course. As well as continuous assessment, each course had a final examination with an examination board which included external examiners from other universities who would also have commented on the course during production. The outcome was a grade and the final degree award was based on the student's overall grade profile. Students were free to choose whichever course they wished; advice was given where appropriate about previous courses that should be studied and where courses qualified for professional recognition a specific course profile would be required.

There was an intense sense of academic and social mission and the way that it was knitted in to the rest of the university system ensured not only high standards but a sense of being part of a whole rather than competitive. Given the high number of students studying a course and its public exposure it was seen as essential that the standards of the course material were high, both academically and pedagogically and to this end it was important to ensure the standards of staff recruited. Much of the material was adopted in other universities to supplement their teaching. And this was a testament to the quality of materials. It was therefore seen as important to provide proper opportunities for research. The period of course design and production was intense and this, combined with the fact that there were no term times, with student vacations providing extra time for research, meant that specific provision needed to be made for adequate research time. Academics were contractually entitled to two months' study leave each year which could be accumulated to a one year's sabbatical. It may be noted that the desire to increase student participation is based on student numbers, not on an increase in research. Interestingly the OU model maintained the importance of research but since there was no limit on the number of students studying a course prepared by a small number of academics the link between student numbers and increased cost of research was broken.

The OU added to the existing diverse system without compromising it. Study centres were typically sited in HE and FE colleges, summer schools on university campuses and part-time staff drawn from across HE. The picture in the 1970s was thus one where conventional universities, polytechnics, the OU, HE and FE colleges concentrated on their various missions and provided opportunities for a variety of needs and talents. Although the new universities created in the 1960s increased opportunities for full-time university study, participation from disadvantaged groups remained stubbornly low. Nevertheless, the OU was typical of the spirit also prevailing in the new universities of high standards within an atmosphere of new ways of thinking about the undergraduate experience. Young academics with a mission to their subject and their community were appointed and given their head.

As we have commented elsewhere, a turning point came with the 1988 Education Act. Although this was concerned mainly with schools, exerting more government control and the beginning of a weakening of local authority responsibilities, these same objectives were also applied to the university system. The University Grants Committee (UGC) was replaced by the University Funding Council whose remit strengthened powers of government over university funding decisions. Academic tenure at universities was weakened. This was followed by the 1992 Act which abolished the polytechnic system by granting all polytechnics university status. The cynic might say that this was a simple solution to the participation problem – suddenly a lot more people were going to university. But as we have commented elsewhere this has led to a reduction of diversity in mission and instead a 'copycat' mentality.

OU funding was also set to change. At its inception it was funded directly by the Department of Education and Science, as was Cranfield University and the Royal College of Art, because their special characteristics made comparison of funding needs difficult. Indeed during the 1970s a special working group was set up by the UGC at the request of the DES to consider including the OU in its remit. The conclusions of this group were that in all academic respects the UGC would welcome the OU but its cost structure was so different that it would be difficult to assess its needs in comparison with other universities. These conclusions were accepted and direct funding continued, with advice to the DES from a 'Visiting Committee' comprising senior figures from universities and business. This decision recognised that not only was the OU mission unique, but that decisions on funding and student numbers were also of a different nature. After the initial period of rapid growth, both in course production and student numbers, by the late 1980s a relatively steady state existed where the costs of writing and rewriting courses (and therefore the number of central academics) was stable and the fixed costs (those not dependent on student numbers) had pretty well plateaued and the marginal cost of increasing student numbers, up to a few thousand, were covered by student fees. This unique position was lost in the early 1990s when the government transferred funding to the UFC and the OU grant was based more closely on average costs per student and therefore assumptions about student numbers.

Another development in the 1980s was the increasing availability of computers in the home, given enormous impetus by the BBC model B computer and its use in schools. Up to this time the thousands of OU students on courses requiring access to computing were able to use terminals at the 156 study centres which were linked by time-sharing to a central mainframe. This was highly innovative at the time of its design in 1969 (although in principle similar to modern cloud computing) but clearly provision now had to be made for access from home. There was great concern about the cost to students at a time when home ownership of computers was by no means as ubiquitous as it is today. But the OU operates on long time scales – a couple of years to write and test a course which might then run for five or more – but the trend was clear. A loan scheme was devised, with the university able to bulk purchase at good prices, together with a discount arrangement with a supplier, Dixons, for those students who wanted to purchase. Because of the rapid development of PCs and Macs at the time there was a problem about what course teams could assume about computer characteristics for a course that would not go live for perhaps another three years and then run for a further five or more. A guess had to be made about what would be available and without specifying a particular machine course teams were given a virtual spec for them to work with – then a recommended machine was chosen nearer the time of presentation.

As ownership of computers in the home became more widespread there was an increased tendency for students to want to communicate with tutors electronically. Interestingly, some research showed that even with this change the maximum size of a tutor group should remain at around 25 for it to work effectively. This pressure presented a threat to the face-to-face tutor sessions, which were a valuable and unique element in the package. Similar threats came from the rise of online courses from other providers and alternatives to broadcast television and radio. In recent years it seems that these threats have been met with attempts to compete with commercial providers on their own terms and abandoning some of its special features, thus weakening the university's USP.

A serious blow to the OU was dealt with the new fees policy. As remarked earlier, fees were low and roughly equal to the marginal costs of more students, but now had to be increased to average cost. This huge increase has led to a massive drop in student numbers and therefore pressure on core costs, notably first on the regional structure and more recently on central academic staff and consequently threatening the course profile unless greater reliance is placed on one-off consultancies, which would again undermine one of the key design features of the university, that it relied on full-time academics, whose own careers depended on the success of the venture. It should be noted that the new fees regime has adversely affected part-time provision across the board; in particular the cost of pursuing a one-off course for pure intellectual interest is likely to mean that they either disappear or become the preserve of the well-off-retired.

The OU has made a significant contribution to participation for students otherwise deprived of or who simply missed out on a university education. Although fees were charged they were low and a fund was available for low income students. It is difficult to make direct comparison with the rest of the system for participation rates because OU students are largely adults (at the beginning solely adults – 18-year-olds were admitted only some years later) and so it is the student's circumstances rather than parental status that is taken into account. But the unique design also made access easier. In the first place there were no entry requirements, the emphasis being on rigorous standards of performance. This was consistent with the fact that students did not sign up for a full degree course; they could just take a one-off course and see how they got on. The option was then available to gradually put together a portfolio which could be recognised for a full degree. Others opted just for one or two select courses, either for self-enrichment or to update themselves or enhance their professional profile. Schoolteachers can take one-off courses to update themselves and to enable them to enrich their own teaching. Many students have moved into the wider university system to do Masters degrees or PhDs, or continuing postgraduate work with the OU. The ability to spread one's programme of study and work from home to suit one's own circumstances was life enhancing for those with demanding jobs, either in paid employment or with childcare responsibilities or who had simply missed out on the opportunity for the conventional university experience. For some it opened the way to a full-time university experience, for others an opportunity to gain a recognised degree-level qualification, often carrying professional accreditation. It has been observed that the presence of a parent struggling at the kitchen table has had positive effects on a child's attitude to study, or even just to reading a book, enriching the life not just of the parent but the family. Although we strongly advocate improving access to the conventional universities there will continue to be an important role for the OU for those who nevertheless find such a route difficult because of other commitments. But for all, whether they have had a full and rich experience at a good university, or whether they have missed out, the contribution to life-long learning it provides as a supplement to opportunities elsewhere should remain a valuable part of the educational scene.

Current policies are seriously threatening the OU, and part-time provision in general, threatening the rich diversity once available. As remarked elsewhere, attempts to introduce a market where everybody plays by the same rules and is measured by the same yardsticks has had the sad effect of reducing opportunity to meet diverse needs. The OU in particular, with its special cost structures, requires a funding mechanism and support that recognises the particular role it can play.

The role of the OU is not just to serve widening participation, but is also a positive support to other parts of the educational sector. We have already discussed how materials prepared by the OU are used elsewhere, and have a 'best practices' effect on teaching throughout the sector. The OU traditionally provides important support to school teachers taking one or two courses a year. This is particularly important in light of the need for enhanced qualifications of mathematics and other STEM teachers. On a more mundane basis, the residential programmes that are a distinctive part of the OU student experience typically occur in the summer and provide an additional financial income to host universities.

A Short Note On: The Case for Career Colleges – The US Model

Lincoln E. Frank

A note on the author

Linc founded Quad Partners, a New York based private equity firm focused exclusively on the education industry, in 2000. Quad's mission is to be the preferred investment partner for owners and management teams – helping them to build great education companies that have a transformative impact on students, teachers, employers, colleges and schools. He has led investments across Quad's portfolio which includes a number of software, tech-enabled service and site-based businesses serving higher education. He holds an LLM from Cambridge University, a JD from the University of Pennsylvania Law School and a BA from Wesleyan University.

Introduction

Given the attempt to create a market for higher education in England and the expressed opinion of government to increase opportunities for private providers, something that is more akin to the North American model than the European model, it is useful to consider the US system. We do this with a particular focus upon 'career colleges' to consider what role private providers can best play in the English system. In the American system, successful private providers are not in competition with traditional universities, but serve a positive role in widening participation in raising skills and employability for disadvantaged individuals in the economy as an alternative to a university course. The system recognises the diversity we think appropriate for English post-18 provision, ranging from apprenticeships through FE colleges through to the elite traditional universities.

At its founding, the United States entertained a debate between traditional higher education and vocational training. Benjamin Franklin, a product of self-education and apprenticeship, argued that the new country required a skilled workforce, with expertise in the trades, to build the economy. He embraced for-profit schools that trained students in surveying, navigation and other skilled trades. These students were not candidates for traditional higher education, which was devoted to the study of theology, Greek and Latin languages, classical literature and philosophy. The 'Latinists' disdained vocational education with 'an unaccountable prejudice in favour of ancient customs and habitudes'.[8]

Higher education in the United States has since grown to comprise the most diverse and largest ecosystem of institutions in the world. There are elite private institutions, both large and small – some exclusively undergraduate colleges, and some research universities with a broad offering of graduate programmes. There are tiny bible colleges and massive state university systems with multiple campuses. Some are wholly residential, some serve commuters, and some are purely online, serving working adults. They are in rural communities and in large cities. Community colleges mostly offer two-year associate degrees with annual full-time student tuition as low as $4,800 for New York City residents at LaGuardia Community College in Queens, while elite private colleges, before the addition of dormitory housing and food service, charge as much as $54,504 per year at Columbia College uptown in Manhattan.

This ecosystem serves the needs of a highly diverse group of students – from 18-year-olds studying history at an elite residential college in an idyllic New England town ('traditional' students) to immigrants working two part-time jobs, learning English and studying accounting at a community college in Brooklyn ('non-traditional' students). Some thrive on massive endowments built up over many years of alumni patronage, while others barely survive on crumbs left over from city and state education budgets. But all depend on Title IV student loan financing from the US federal government, a programme emanating from the post-Second World War GI Bill and comprised of needs-based grants and loans.

Then there are for-profit career colleges, training students for careers in nursing, allied health, cosmetology, aesthetics, welding, coding, truck driving and other skilled trades and professions. At their best, these colleges offer programmes that are directly tied to available jobs in the communities they serve, often for jobs requiring licensure from trade groups or governmental organisations. They reverse-engineer the skill sets required for these jobs, incorporate them into focused education taught by practitioners of the trade or profession, prepare the students to pass required licensure examinations, and help to place the graduates in jobs. They mostly attract non-traditional higher education students – first to attend college in their families, immigrants, working adults, single parents, lower income urban or rural individuals. The most effective career colleges understand the challenges and needs of these students and, in addition to the academics, address basic work skills – how to dress, interact with co-workers, write a resume, shake hands, show up on time and every day – as well as attending to the life events that get in the way of fulfilling a programme – lack of funds for commuting fares or childcare, illness, abusive partners, history of failure.

At their worst, these colleges do the opposite. They educate students in general subjects or ones for which there are limited jobs, they charge excessive tuition fees, saddling students with compromising debt, they suffer low graduation rates, and offer programmes that are longer than required. In sum, the good ones offer focused programmes with a great value proposition to the appropriate students, while the bad ones offer studies that are mismatched to both the economy and the solicited student population.

Benjamin Franklin's debate continues between those favouring traditional non-profit higher education and proponents of alternative higher education. Of course, the answer is not one or the other, but both with diverse higher education alternatives offered to all who seek participation in the developed world's twenty-first century skill-based economy. For some careers, longer intellectually intensive degree programmes in traditional college settings are best. For others, shorter skill-based non-degree offerings are the ticket. Importantly, which career and which preparation is also determined by the student – his or her intellectual capacity, rigour, ambition, goals, financial means, and life circumstances. Addressing these student differences honestly and transparently is necessary to design the right higher education programmes. Clear disclosure of student outcomes and cost will allow students to choose the most appropriate ones for them.

What follows is an argument for the role of for-profit career colleges, but only if they are effective, ethical and transparent. Many have not been, and clear, thoughtful and appropriate regulation is required to ensure quality.

Skills-based careers

While all jobs require some kind of expertise, many can be learned 'on the job'. This is true for house painting, sales, janitorial, manufacturing, food service and numerous business jobs – some are higher paying positions with potential upward mobility that require an undergraduate degree for employment and some are modestly paid with limited opportunity for advancement requiring no higher education. Some jobs require years of skill-based training and licensure – doctors, lawyers, engineers, architects, accountants. Others require shorter, focused training and licensure – nurses, cosmetologists, aestheticians, truck drivers, massage therapists, allied health practitioners, plumbers, electricians, welders.

In the US, traditional higher education fills the needs for job seekers in fields requiring the prestige of an undergraduate degree – as an indicator of intellect, rigour, or, some fear, social and economic background – and existing graduate studies address a number of advanced professional jobs, such as lawyers and doctors. However, skills-based jobs requiring shorter, more focused training are largely ignored by traditional higher education. The sector neither is interested in, nor capable of delivering such vocational programmes. This education is the purview of purpose driven career colleges, most of which are for-profit.

The successful career colleges are wholly oriented on student outcomes, and begin with an analysis of available jobs and requisite skills:

- Are there available skilled jobs in the community for well-trained graduates?
- Did the graduate get one of those jobs?
- Has the student learned the skills necessary to perform that job?
- Did the student pass the required licensure exam, if applicable?
- Did the student complete the programme?
- Was the programme designed to accomplish these outcomes in the shortest period of time?
- Were only the students likely to succeed enrolled in the programme?

The best career colleges substitute for the old-time apprenticeship system. They match the unemployed, or under-employed, with employers. They focus only on the skills required for the job, design programmes in collaboration with local employers, and incorporate job internships. They depend on adjunct faculty that work in the field of study bringing up-to-date, real world training to their students. They inspire students with a narrative of success and provide milestones of accomplishment. But, given the 'non-traditional' demographic they serve, they must do more than that.

Student services: retention and job placement

This is where honesty and transparency are required in the conversation. The truth is that young adults whose parents have graduated from college, who have gone to good secondary schools, and who have been raised with expectations for achievement, are likely to attend traditional institutions of higher education and pursue a certain realm of careers. Those from lower income families whose parents did not attend college, immigrants, students graduating from underachieving secondary schools, dropouts, part-time workers and children of single parents are often poorly served by traditional colleges, even if they could achieve admittance.

These 'non-traditional' students often require targeted student services in order for them to be successful in higher education. Reading textbooks, listening to lectures, and doing homework in the library may not be sufficiently engaging for them. Many have a background of failure in their academic and employment pursuits and may be prone to giving in to that history when challenged. And, life gets in the way – boyfriends cause trouble, childcare fails, they don't have sufficient money for commuting fares, they get sick. Traditional higher education would deem these issues beyond its responsibility. However, career colleges must recognise, confront, and solve them to deliver the successful student outcomes outlined earlier.

Community colleges in the US typically offer two-year associate degrees and serve a similar demographic to for-profit career colleges. They are government funded and charge tuition fees equal to the usual grant provided by the federal government for lower income students. However, they graduate only 20 per cent of their students over three years for a two-year programme. Why? Students get lost in large classes and need to wait for desired courses to be offered. In addition, life gets in the way and many community colleges are not equipped to intervene. In order to maintain the accreditation required to access federal student tuition support, for-profit career colleges must achieve specified graduation rates.

As a result, they provide student resources that are 'off the grid' for traditional higher education. If a student misses a class, they don't get docked a grade. Rather, the teacher is responsible to call/ email/text them. 'I missed you in class today. Is everything okay? Can you come in for a make-up session?' Campus staff may lend them bus money or introduce classmates who have cars. If one day is missed, it's easier to miss the next. In fact, the embarrassment of another (and often expected) failure, may prevent the student from returning to school.

Early recognition, empathetic outreach, and a shared responsibility for retention among all faculty and staff characterise these institutions. This results in retention rates which can be meaningfully higher for similar demographics (in many cases, even more challenged demographics) than at cafeteria style community colleges. Retention is everyone's responsibility at these schools. How many educators and staff at traditional colleges view their jobs in this way? How many 'chief retention officers' exist in traditional college/university settings?

Course design also is important to student success. Programmes in other settings might frontload the course of study with the fundamentals to be memorised and tested before moving on to the practical components of the studies. 'Of course! That's the proper design of a programme', a typical university professor would reply. 'We get the boring bits out of the way first.' It also serves to sort out the students who are unlikely to thrive in the programme. That's not how a programme is properly designed in a career college focused on graduation, because early failure, premature testing, and boring lectures result in unnecessary dropouts. They start with practical topics, hands-on work, smaller and more engaging increments of study – all clearly linked to getting and performing the intended job. With these building blocks of academic success and interest – and having developed peer and faculty relationships and incorporated the day-to-day logistics of getting to school, studying and balancing their lives – the students are more likely to persevere and learn the fundamentals and 'boring bits' when later introduced and their necessity has become more apparent.

Graduation without a job is a failure for students in career colleges – and existential for the colleges themselves. (US parents of students in expensive traditional colleges are beginning to say the same and questioning the value proposition of these institutions versus less expensive state schools, but that is a topic for another article.) These colleges begin job placement as soon as the student enrols. What is the job like, what is expected of the employee, how to write a resume, how to act in an interview, how to relate with peers, how to respond to bosses. They are introduced to role models who come to speak, and often are the adjunct instructors in class. There may be dressing closets with suits, ties, shirts, dresses and blouses appropriate for interviews. Work training is integrated into the programme of study – often on potential employer sites. This makes a student more confident in interviewing, more capable in the field, and may directly result in a job.

These colleges have dedicated staff who develop relationships with local employers and arrange internships. They solicit them for job openings, set up graduating student interviews and promote their candidates. They make sure the student is prepared for the interview, is dressed appropriately, knows how to get there and actually shows up. They follow up with the employer to answer questions and advocate for the student. They provide an important feedback loop to those that design and teach the programmes – what were employer issues with candidates or hired students, what were they well-prepared for and what were the deficiencies. This is critical to both hiring and ultimate career success. Contrast this with a traditional college's career office where potential jobs are posted on index cards pinned to bulletin boards – actual or digital.

Retention and job placement are in the DNA of effective career schools. It is their mission to graduate students and get them a job. Hopefully, that is because those working in these schools care deeply for their students and are well attuned to their challenges. Some would argue that it is merely self-preservation because the schools lose their access to student tuition funding if they do not achieve certain graduation and job placement metrics. In a business world starved of ethical values that view may be understood, but there is something to be said for a funding system that encourages good behaviour.

Regulation and student tuition funding

The financial model underpinning higher education in the US is provided under Tile IV of the Higher Education Act of 1965. It derives from the highly successful GI Bill enacted in 1944 which provided tuition and living expense payments for returning veterans to pursue traditional college or vocational programmes. Title IV has been re-authorised and tweaked many times over the years, but its fundamental role has not changed. It is the first source for students to access financial aid to pay tuition and living expenses, at colleges, universities and vocational schools – traditional and for-profit – in the US. Next are college scholarships, typically funded out of endowment funds, and then parents. Title IV involves a mix of grants (Pell grants) plus subsidised and unsubsidised loans. The amounts available and loan repayment provisions have evolved with different borrower choices, deferral options, and, more recently, the inclusion of income-based repayment formulas. The entire programme is based on the financial wherewithal of the student and his or her family. Grants are available only for families with lower economic means. The awarding of subsidised loans also is means tested, as is the applicable interest rate and repayment terms.

In order to qualify for its students to access Title IV, the college must be accredited by a federally approved group. There are two types – regional, which mostly accredit traditional colleges and some higher degree-granting for-profit schools, and national, which accredit vocational and most for-profit colleges. Each is a self-governing organisation with dedicated staff, but boards and visiting commissions made up of representatives from the related accredited institutions. Both types have standards related to faculty credentials, resources and financial stability. While regional accreditation is more prestigious, once accredited, an institution is not required to achieve student success benchmarks relating to graduation or job attainment. National accreditors, however, have strict rules around such measures, in addition to others related to advertising, enrolment, programme design and other criteria.

One of the leading national accreditors, ACCSC (the Accrediting Commission of Career Schools and Colleges) requires a graduation rate of 60 per cent for nine-month programmes, 55 per cent for 12-month, and 40 per cent for two or more years. These typically are full year courses of study – no summers off. Vocational students need to get to employment as soon as possible. In addition, substantial time off can lead to dropping out. ACCSC requires employment rates of 70 per cent and for programmes educating students for jobs with mandated government licensure, students must pass the related exams at a 70 per cent rate. If a programme fails or a college overall is underperforming, it may be put on warning and, if the metrics do not improve, lose its accreditation for that programme or altogether. The accreditors may take into account the particular demographics of students served or the importance of filling certain critical jobs in a community in determining the ramifications for failure to meet the standards.

The federal government imposes additional requirements on for-profit colleges that do not apply to traditional institutions. These include student default rates on Title IV loans below specific levels, and receipt of at least 10 per cent of revenues from other than

Title IV sources. In addition, colleges with concerning financial stability or operations may be required to post a letter of credit to the Department of Education in case the institution fails. While there are a host of other reporting obligations and requirements for participation in Title IV, the key student outcomes metrics are the graduation and placement rates set by the accrediting bodies and the student loan default rates. They address the four big indicators of student success: 1) Was the programme designed and taught in a compelling manner with attendant student services and only offered to students likely to persist? – Graduation Rate, 2) Did the programme effectively train students for the jobs intended and in communities where such jobs were available? – Employment Rate, 3) If a licensure exam is required in order to work in the related field, did the programme prepare the student to pass? – Licensure Exam Pass Rate, and 4) Did the student persist in the career field and achieve sufficient success in order to service their student loans? – Loan Default Rate.

The role of for-profit institutions

In many halls of traditional higher education, for-profit providers are, at best, derided as inferior institutions lacking in intellect, culture and rigour. At worst, they are accused of preying on students with limited options, providing inadequate and expensive education unrelated or insufficient for employment, and, ultimately, saddling the failed students with life compromising debt. There has been some truth in these accusations. However, because of the inherent condescension of traditional higher education to vocational or career training and its inability to service the needs of non-traditional students, for-profit institutions have filled, and should continue to fill, the void left by the traditional sector. But, they must be required to satisfy certain indications of student success.

The Great Recession proved a case study for the good and bad of for-profit higher education. When unemployment began to spike in 2008, those in unskilled jobs suffered the most. For minorities, and those with only a high school diploma, unemployment rose to 16 per cent in 2009 versus 10 per cent overall. Young adults sought out higher education to get the skills they needed to secure the jobs available in a poor economy. The traditional sector was ill-equipped to respond to this need. They were capacity constrained and not interested in vocational training. The for-profits jumped in, first with core career-focused programmes and then with longer degree programmes often in generalised areas (business or marketing) or in fields with limited employment opportunities (graphic design and psychology) – all fuelled by the federal government's provision of Title IV tuition funding.

Students graduating from properly designed programmes aligned with available skilled employment opportunities enjoyed success. The others did not. They graduated, or dropped out of, longer and more expensive programmes with no resulting job and sizable debt on which many defaulted. Only in hindsight with cohort graduation and employment rates below standards, would the programmes and colleges be declared failing by their accreditors and forced to be discontinued or close. The result could have been anticipated. It was like the sub-prime mortgage bubble and bust. What started as a good idea (government supported mortgage lending for responsible potential homeowners) turned into a massive abuse and nightmare for borrowers: subprime loans with deceptive terms marketed to inappropriate borrowers.

For-profits entities are good at identifying unserved areas of opportunity and the profit motive allows them to attract the necessary capital. There is little disagreement that trained skills are required to participate fully in the twenty-first century knowledge-based economy and that many people on the other side of this skills gap are being left behind. How do we address this? Some say that the government should establish skills-based programmes. How do they know what is needed in a particular locality? Others suggest that employers should establish their own apprenticeship programmes to train workers. They should, but haven't on any scale. Perhaps community colleges should be provided with more resources. They should, but only on the condition that they build the student services required to attain appropriate graduation and employment rates. What about traditional higher education? Shouldn't that sector begin to serve the career training needs of the non-traditional student? It can't; it doesn't have the interest, expertise or resources, and in any case it has a different mission.

For-profits can fill the gap as long as government regulation of graduation, employment, default rates and prospective student disclosure protects against rogue traders. As for-profits, they will pursue profit by refining their business models to meet the needs of students. With profits, additional capital will flow, superior management will be attracted, and higher quality institutions will emerge.

7

Adjusting to the Future

In each chapter to this point, we have analysed shortcomings in the current university funding arrangements, but have stopped just at the point of making policy recommendations. This is because we have wanted to bring everything together in constructing holistic policies.

The objectives of changes of policy initiated by the Browne Report were:

1. to improve participation and in particular access from less advantaged groups;
2. to improve quality and student choice in a diverse system by creating a market leading to competition.

We believe that creating a market was neither necessary nor desirable in achieving the stated aims, which we otherwise completely support. However, we have taken the regime change on its own terms and will continue to do so in this chapter. It is for the government of the day to determine the funding regime, and the current government clearly supports the market elements arising from the Browne review.

Our problem is that the manner in which the Browne Report was implemented and the way in which subsequent policy has developed has led to a failure to achieve the stated objectives. The system constructed is simply inefficient in its inability to encourage competition and in how it rewards failure. Further, it has encouraged micromanagement of and within universities to the detriment of the traditional focus on the academic esprit that has been essential to the high standing traditionally enjoyed by our Higher Education system. In the following, we present clear and concrete policies that follow recommendations made (for example) by Browne. Further, everything is not only 'costed' but we impose the rigorous rule that additional support from the taxpayer cannot be provided at this time. The sector has done extremely well in funding over the period of national austerity, and the priorities lie elsewhere.

The hierarchy of universities

The economics model of marriage is based upon the idea of 'assortative matching', where individuals of similar standing in characteristics form relationships. This model can be applied more widely and is relevant to universities. Suppose there are good and weak students. If learning is 'complementary', putting the good students together and the weak students together produces more learning than if there are two mixed groups. In this world, it is efficient to match together the good students. But, even if it is not efficient, this may be the outcome on the basis of individual interest. If the good students benefit from interacting with each other, they may prefer to work together even if the weak students could gain immensely from interaction. By 'good' we are using a shorthand in what follows for the highly focused academic qualities sought by traditional universities. This is not to imply negativity to other talents and abilities or the difficulty of identifying the 'good' and the 'weak' or the possible potential of a 'weak' student. But it shows a further reason why self-interest may not lead to efficient outcomes in this sector and why the sector is so very hierarchical.

The change to an uncapped, high fee system has actually increased the hierarchical nature of universities rather than leading to the intended competition across universities. This is for two reasons. The ability to expand has meant that a greater proportion of good students can go to a limited number of universities. The top universities can cream off the good students. But in addition, for reasons we have stated in Chapter Three, universities below the top have tended to go down-market, taking students from the next lower stage in the hierarchy. This has led to grade inflation and lowering of tariffs as marketing tools and the weakening of the academic content of programmes. The relative advantage to a good student of going to a top university has risen. In the past, an advisor could argue to a student that University X was better for their needs and interests than higher-ranked University Y. University X might be in a better location for them, have extracurricular provision that fits well with the student's interests in music or the sports, or have particular programmes that match the student's interests. But now it is hard to advise a student to turn down a place at a Russell Group university to go elsewhere.

This means that there is also now an increased payoff to being considered a top university rather than just a good university. For this reason, it is not surprising that the Russell Group developed itself as an extremely effective marketing tool. Politicians and the media, and consequently parents and students have come to believe that the Group comprises all of the top universities in the UK. In its marketing publication 'Profile', the Group emphasises the network externalities we have described – 'our students benefit from working with and learning from a highly-motivated and talented peer group'.

Prior to the changes in the funding regime, a second group of top universities existed. The '1994 Group' was founded in the same year as the Russell Group and was made up of universities with very strong research records that most would have seen as indistinguishable from the Russell Group. The main distinguishing factor was size and the original members of the Russell Group typically had medical schools and large engineering departments. The 1994 Group members were on the whole smaller universities based on a single campus offering high-class research and teaching in a collegiate atmosphere. But with the increased returns to establishing a place at the top of the hierarchy, individual members of the 1994 Group sought membership with the Russell Group. When the Russell Group admitted 1994 Group members Durham, Exeter, Queen Mary and York in 2012, the 1994 Group became unsustainable as a second group seeking to distinguish itself as also being leading research universities, and it disbanded.

A further group of top schools and colleges (that could demarcate themselves separately as universities) are those of the University of London. The University of London had developed as a more interlocked group than the Russell Group or the 1994

Group, with some quality control exercised across the colleges and some significant university facilities such as the Senate House Library. Imperial College left the University of London in 2007 and the university became decentralised well before the change in fee regime. More recently, City University joined the University of London, an indication of the value of the brand name.

While the University of London has diminished in effectiveness, it has not followed the 1994 Group and disbanded. The University of London contains the large Colleges: Queen Mary (Russell), City, Goldsmiths, SOAS, Birkbeck, UCL (Russell), LSE (Russell), Kings (Russell), Royal Holloway and the specialist Royal Veterinary College, the London School of Hygiene and Tropical Medicine and St Georges Medical School. The simple fact is that, for a College in the Russell Group, the University of London name carries little additional weight. The options were either to form a grouping of common purpose among the non-Russell colleges, or to have a diminished and secondary University of London that weights the preferences of the Russell Group members. The outcome was the second option, leaving the non-Russell Group members only marginally better off than non-Russell, non-University of London universities of comparable stature. This is an example of the inefficiencies of the current funding regime. The internationally recognised brand of the 'University of London' is being downgraded, affecting the recruitment of overseas students for whom the 'University of London' degree has traditionally had high cachet.

The extremely good non-Russell universities formerly in the 1994 Group or still within the University of London complain that life is unfair, that they are just as good as the Russell Group universities. This unfortunately fails to understand the nature of clubs such as the Russell Group. You are admitted to a club not because you'd like to be, or out of fairness, but because it is in the interest of the existing members. The standard economic theory of clubs is that there are fixed costs – for example, the costs of maintaining the club building – and adding another member allows these to be spread more widely. This was pertinent to the University of London, with its central Library and Administrative facilities, but is less pertinent to the Russell Group. Indeed, in some ways the raison d'être of the Russell Group is to somewhat arbitrarily take a portion of the good universities and self-certify some of them as 'elite' to give them a competitive advantage – there would be little point in this unless some good competitors were in effect 'declassified', making it harder for them to compete. Indeed, a cynical view is that the Russell Group admitted just enough universities to force the disbandment of the 1994 Group and even weaken the University of London. We wonder whether or not it was wise for the remaining 1994 Group universities to disband the organisation, given that it gave them a common voice in consultations such as the current review of Higher Education. Certainly, the post-1992 universities have gained a voice through their organisation, MillionPlus.

This somewhat long-winded discussion leads to the simple conclusion that the Russell Group universities have become disproportionate to the sector due to essentially network externalities. Their student numbers have grown massively at the expense of the very good universities next down in the hierarchy. This is economically inefficient but also damages the very brand of 'elite' that the Russell Group seeks to establish. Further, the dominance of this group effectively destroys rather than enhances competition. One way forward is to impose individual or group caps just for these universities. By limiting their student numbers, we would give other universities 'room to breathe'. However, as we discuss below, we think that there are other policies that better integrate the objective of restoring competition with effective mechanisms for widening participation.

Restoring competition

As we have described in Chapter Three, there is effectively no financial incentive to compete for the best students in the current framework. A university in the next tier below the Russell Group could have used the additional funding to cut its student–staff ratio (SSR) and otherwise enhance the academic value of its offering. It has been easier, and less costly, to simply go down the demand curve and admit students with lower entry points.

Browne gave a perfectly plausible mechanism for establishing competition – cap the overall number of students so that universities have to compete for students. In Chapter Three, we showed that under this regime, universities would find it effective to compete for top students. Consider, for example, the position of the LSE and other universities in London with good economics programmes. Even without the benefit of NSS (National Student Survey) scores and the TEF (Teaching Excellence Framework), prospective students know that – if they go to the LSE – they will likely be taught by PhD students and not by world-famous professors. As we have argued above, a good student will still be inclined to go to the LSE since they get to interact with other good students, even leaving aside the prestige of the LSE degree. Now suppose that one of the other London universities ups its game in Economics by significantly lowering its SSR and in other academic ways. Some good students will now be more on the margin between the LSE and this other university. The LSE, provided that the numbers of students involved are not too large, will not incur the costs of increasing its focus upon undergraduate teaching, which would involve doing so for all its students. The other university will therefore be able to 'poach' a limited number of top students away from the LSE and under the principle of assortative matching this would attract further top students.

That whole story relied upon two things – the other university, ranked lower in the hierarchy than the LSE, has to engage in real expenditure on academic aspects of the programme, and – even then – cannot be too ambitious in the number of students it is seeking to attract. In effect, the second university becomes a 'boutique' university, smaller in size and offering an experience tailored to a limited market. We think this is analogous to the hotel market. Depending upon one's desired expenditure level, there are hotel chains ranging from the Mandarin Oriental and the Four Seasons, working down through intermediate ranges of the Hiltons and Marriotts, before going to the Premier Inns. The brand name provides a labelling of the expected quality and level of services in the different hotels. But there remains a market for niche, boutique hotels of every quality and price level. Further, the Mandarin Oriental is not too bothered if a small boutique five-star hotel opens nearby and takes away a small number of its customers.

We expect that, once a system is set up that requires competition and universities realise that they have to compete and can no longer pile up lots of less-qualified students, we will move away from the 'cookie cutter' approach that has been adopted in the current environment. One of the most dispiriting features of the current markets without competition is that everyone is seeking to be in the same space and this is encouraged by league tables, where everybody is ranked by the same criteria. As we have commented, at present the only way to move up the tables is to mimic those above so that they encourage uniformity rather than the aim of diversity. Restoration of competition means that each university needs to find its niche, to find its USP.

During the Second World War, German artistic emigres landed at Black Mountain College in North Carolina. This obscure institution became the place to be for modern art and music. In England, Morley College in Lambeth had Gustav Holst as its Music Director, a post subsequently taken by Michael Tippett. Currently, London South Bank University is the home of the National Bakery School. If you want to hire apprentices for your bakery or restaurant, LSBU is the place to look. As you go through the list of universities in England, each institution jumps out as having particular strengths. Goldsmiths is the university of the Young British Artists, SOAS has its focus on ethnography, Birkbeck provides evening education of the highest quality. Everybody knows of the specialist work of the London School of Hygiene and Tropical Medicine and the Royal Agricultural College (now University). In these ways, each institution should strive to be among the best in a particular field.

Some universities, notably the former polytechnics, while having areas of research strength, are in general more focused on teaching quality. Without an expensive research overhead, these universities can operate on a lower cost basis than other, research-intensive institutions. The Browne proposals, and government expectations, were that universities would engage in price competition. However, participants in the sector considered this highly unlikely, since lowering the price would be taken as a signal of lower quality. Even if that were not the case, each university has some monopoly power and will not want to lower fees for all students in order to attract a few more. We propose to mitigate this factor by offering universities two fee options, where the university can either set the base fee (to be discussed below) or it can set a reduced fee, with additional support provided by a central grant per student making up a significant part of the fee differential. We will come back to this when we discuss the situation from the perspective of students.

The government has emphasised the potential role for private providers. Based upon the US experience described in Chapter Six, this should be limited to 'career colleges' that are tightly regulated and subject to external professional examinations. We see potential expansion of private providers in the traditional university sector as lessening quality competition, not raising it. If private providers take over 'bread-and-butter' provision in low-cost subjects such as Business Studies – a reliable source of income for universities – this just means that student fees for high-cost subjects will have to go up. We take the same view as the BMA does on private contracts in the NHS – they are a costly diversion from the main business of the health service, taking away more straightforward and risk free procedures, leaving expensive and more difficult cases for the specialists in the NHS.

QAA, NSS, TEF and all that

We have a clear proposal here. This is that the NSS and TEF should be discontinued, and that the functions of the QAA should be to assure quality in the sense of the validity of degrees through the examination process, notably by restoring the effectiveness of the external examination system, and to have a continuing role in assuring that systems for sound governance are in place.

League tables, based in part upon the NSS, have become extremely misleading. Our particular concern is that the great impact of these will be on the least informed potential students. A recent Guardian league table, which gives a strong weighting to NSS scores, headlines that Nottingham Trent University has overtaken the University of Nottingham. From the description, Nottingham Trent has undertaken significant steps towards improving quality of teaching. Except, however, in special circumstances, like it or not, few schoolteachers would recommend that a student offered a place at both attends Nottingham Trent instead of the University of Nottingham unless it offered a course of particular interest to the student. This is partly because of potential employer perception but, one has to say, also how the universities attended by their students affects the publicity and standing of secondary schools.

The NSS is intended to be a consumer satisfaction measure in the sense that Tripadvisor is a consumer satisfaction measure. If one looks up town centre hotels in Leeds on Tripadvisor, the top three hotels are expensive boutique properties. But the fourth is a mid-range aparthotel and the fifth is a Premier Inn. The listing is simply not comparing like-for-like. The top-rated Dakota Deluxe is not the right place to take a family with young kids, and the Premier Inn is not the ideal base for a romantic honeymoon. Those using Tripadvisor generally understand this. Before the flow of information on the internet and elsewhere, there may have been a point in government ratings of university teaching and student satisfaction, just as governments could rate hotels one star through to five stars. It should be noted however that the star rating for hotels was primarily about facilities available and not the quality of the service, which was left to private printed guidebooks. We have argued elsewhere that in any case the NSS is unreliable even on its own terms.

The TEF, like the access agreements for the OFFA (Office for Fair Access), seems mostly to involve considerable essay writing by senior administrators and marking by central assessors. We simply fail to see the point. We'd like our students, not our most senior administrators, to write essays.

When we began, we said that we saw the role for regulation to be similar to the airline industry. The government needs to ensure safety – in the case of universities, the validity of the degrees awarded. It doesn't have to set standards on the quality of the food served during the flight. In the same way, once the government through the QAA has restored the external examiner system and ensured that universities have sufficient governance to run their own business, the government should step out of the way and not micromanage. The remaining role can be through the OIA, which provides an effective ombudsman system to consider and record student complaints. The OIA, as currently, can also disseminate best practice through their workshops and publications.

In our view, the greatest beneficiaries of the restoration of the external examiner system would be the universities just below the Russell Group, who have traditionally offered research and teaching and standards comparable to Russell Group universities. It is precisely the grade inflation devaluing the meaning of a first- and upper second-class degree that has forced students to seek to go to a Russell Group university, even when another university offered a programme better tailored to their interests. We have argued that the external system needs to be restored by increasing remuneration and responsibilities of external examiners, not by writing bureaucratic descriptions of what a degree entails and providing online training for less experienced academics to fulfil the role. Externals should be senior, experienced academics whose standing is unquestionable and views respected.

Funding

The move away from the block teaching grant to income following student choice in the form of fees, is the foundation of having a market. As we have said on regular occasions throughout the book, and repeat again, we would not have gone in that direction. That is, however, a matter for the government of the day, so we have considered the system on its own terms. In that light, our proposals are to make the system work by restoring competition and otherwise achieving the stated aims more efficiently.

We see no reason why the base fee should not be set at roughly the cost of production, which – as Browne noted in 2010 – was then around £6000 per student. We have pointed out in Chapter Four that, for non-profits, surplus income is spent according to the preferences of dominant stakeholders. The increase in teaching funding of about 50 per cent – by setting fees at £9000 instead of the £6000 cost base – has coincided (and perhaps to some extent caused) greater managerialism in universities, an over-weighting of the preferences of senior administrators compared to those of academics and students. This has, in our view, caused additional distortions and inefficiencies in the use of taxpayers' funds. In any case, setting fees that far above the cost of production has overly encouraged universities to admit students who might not be best qualified or matched to the programmes on offer.

Figures show that universities have increased recurrent spend on students by about 20 per cent since the increase in fees. Either on a transitional or ongoing basis, that reality might mean that the appropriate cost basis is now around £7000–£7500. Recall however that universities were explicitly advised that fee levels above £6000 were predicated upon spending (at least 30 per cent of the differential above £6000) on widening participation. If widening participation is indeed a government priority we would expect universities to 'earn back' any fee level above £6000 by actually meeting targets for widening participation, not just agreeing plans with OFFA. Even then, we cannot see why the fee cap should not be lowered to the recurrent cost per student of £7000–£7500.

We have already indicated that some universities, with lower costs, might have a different fee level, as in the original Browne proposals and government expectations. Many of the post-1992 universities have lower cost bases, since they are not incurring the heavy costs of research at the international level for much of their subject offering. While university research is intended to be funded independently through the QR grant following on from the REF exercise, and from the research councils and indeed corporate and charitable foundation grants, in practice much falls upon the student. Insofar as there is research-led teaching, it is not unreasonable that, as at present, the student covers some of the research cost. It is noted that good universities generally consider 40 per cent of the time of the academic as spent on research, comparable to the time spent on teaching (the remaining on administration). This is already incorporated in the proposed base fee levels of £7000–£7500. High cost subjects requiring laboratories for teaching as well as research would continue to receive additional grant funding.

We can therefore envisage a system where, in addition to the base fee, there is a lower fee (perhaps £5000) at universities with less of a focus upon research. The choice between fee regime could be up to the university, with a block grant of perhaps £1000–£1250 per student making up a substantial part (in our example, half) of any loss due to the lowered fee. It is noted that some of these universities already effectively charge less through 'hidden discounts' of financial support to students. The university choosing the lower fee option would benefit from greater student demand, which they could use to adopt greater selectivity in the students admitted. Universities adopting this approach would make clear that although they do research, the reason for lower fees is their concentration on teaching and that this is reflected in their course profile. This allows the university to run more efficiently at still lower cost, and helps these universities to restore their reputations for high quality teaching and a distinctive course offering and, for example, taking an active role in supporting the need for more high-quality apprenticeships in partnerships with employers.

What is vital however is that any fee differential should not have a negative impact on widening participation at the top universities. Given what we perceive to be a greater price sensitivity on the part of students from lower income households, lower fees at some universities could unduly influence the choice of university. This risk would be reduced with a well-designed system of means testing for fees and maintenance awards, which we in any case favour over the current contingent-repayment loans system on grounds of economic efficiency as well as fairness, together with our proposals below for university caps tied to widening participation.

There currently remains some funding for block teaching grants. So a mechanism exists within Office for Students (OfS) to expand this to be used directly to incentivise universities to meet the objectives set by the government. One of these is widening participation. But also, as at present, different subjects can be prioritised. We have already discussed the irony that everyone jumps to saying that STEM subjects need support, when in fact there is good reason to think that currently out of favour subjects such as Modern Languages are the ones where the funding could better, or at least also, be directed.

We have great difficulty, on multiple grounds, with a system where subsidies take the form predominantly of forgiving debt when the investment turns out (from a financial point of view) poorly. On our rough assumption of 50 per cent non-repayment of student loans, the taxpayer is currently subsidising half of the £9000 fee, or £4500 per student. We think that these funds can be used much more directly and effectively, without rewarding failure in the way of the current system. If competition between universities is restored, and if education quality results from this competition, the remaining policy goal is to widen participation. We discuss below how best to use the funding to achieve this aim.

Student fees and loans

We are bemused why it is thought that we should charge the highest fees in Europe (in Denmark, to take an extreme example, all education is free, from generous nursery provision through to university) and, in particular, to charge fees in excess of the historical costs of university. We note that at present universities claim to spend around £1000 per student per annum on widening participation schemes which they put forward to OFFA. We will propose that the widening participation funds can better be spent on means-tested fees and maintenance awards. A first reduction of fee levels from £9000 to £8000, combined with the ending of the OFFA process as now designed, should therefore have no impact on the university balance sheet. The remaining reduction we contemplate to £7500 or £7000 would be a real reduction in unit funding.

There are good arguments for lowering fees as far as £6000 to reflect the historical cost of teaching and student support. The strongest counter-argument for fees higher than that – up to £7000 or £7500 – is that universities have increased the cost base by about 20 per cent due to higher expenditures on staffing and direct educational resources such as teaching rooms. We do not understand why expenditures in all recurrent categories have increased by roughly the same percentage, some of which do not reflect a commitment to improving the student experience for the students actually paying the fees. We note the recent *Student academic experience survey* undertaken by the Higher Education Policy Institute (HEPI).[1] While 'value for money' perceptions have improved from a low base, still only 35 per cent of students in England perceive 'good or very good' value. Students rate spending on teaching facilities (65 per cent) and teaching staff (60 per cent) as the most reasonable use of their money.

We question the logic in charging current students for the Student Centres and other luxury buildings, aimed more at attracting potential students rather than improving the educational experience, that have characterised university plans over the last few years. It is unlikely that a typical student would value access to a University Student Centre (as opposed to the Sports Centre) at much more than £100 a year. We have also commented on the unfairness of students having to pay for projects that will be enjoyed not by them but by future cohorts. If some universities have borrowed large sums to pay for facilities such as this, there is a legitimate issue of how and whether those universities would be able to survive or prosper in a lowered income regime. Neither equity nor economic efficiency, however, supports loading these costs onto current student fees.

Let us suppose in the first instance that fees are set to £7500. We can see no reason why the government seeks to make a large profit on the interest rates charged on student loans. Long-term borrowing costs for the government currently entail a negative real interest rate (the long-term rate is less than the rate of inflation), so even a zero real interest rate would more than cover the cost of finance. As we have discussed, we also see the current system of forgiveness of loans after 30 years as 'rewarding failure'. We begin therefore by looking at a possible loan system with a real interest rate of zero and no loan forgiveness (except in extreme cases of disability or death).

The best structuring of these loans, we would suggest, is as a 'mortgage' provided by the government in order to pay for university. If this mortgage runs over a normal career of 40 years, and was repaid at a uniform rate as with a typical repayment mortgage (but with fixed real rather than pound sterling repayments), a total fees mortgage amount of £22,500 (based upon £7500 per annum) would cost about £50 a month in current pounds. It is hard to see that this is unduly burdensome for anyone with a university degree. It is also a form of borrowing which is well understood. The same individuals who are taking out a university loan currently up to £60,000 may also soon be contemplating a further, more significant burden of a mortgage on properties of several hundred thousand pounds. In principle, therefore, properly supported student loans are feasible if the repayment system is rationalised along the mortgage model at a zero real rate of interest.

It is only the high fees, high current interest rates and the nature of the current repayment scheme that turns the monthly repayments into a large sum. If someone has a student loan of £60,000 but has to subsidise non-repayment by other students and pay an interest rate of 6.1 per cent, then the mortgage repayments become significant. Just the interest rate of 6.1 per cent rather than the rate of inflation (currently 3.1 per cent) significantly increases the repayment amount each month. Adding in cross-subsidisation of non-repayment, and the amount becomes even higher. The burden becomes so high that the taxpayer is left with an unpaid debt at the end of the 30-year forgiveness period of about 50 per cent. This simply and obviously does not make sense.

It may be felt that, even with repayments in the region of £100 a month on a £50,000 student loan (for fees and maintenance) at a zero real interest rate, this could be burdensome for someone on a low income. There might be a case for *ex post* redistribution on the basis that everyone should be insured against the possibility that their student experience has proven – at least financially – unprofitable. Even then, it is hard to see why the insurance and redistribution associated with student loans should differ from that already built into the income tax system. Currently, low income households pay a low or zero income tax, and rates are then set progressively. Rather than constructing a cumbersome contingent-repayment loan system, why not have a straightforward graduate tax as a surcharge on income tax payments, with a rate set to achieve repayment on average? Of course, this cuts the psychological link to the idea of having a loan rather than a tax surcharge. A way of maintaining the link, but largely using the insurance and redistribution inherent in the tax system, is to make repayments on a cohort basis. When the cohort has repaid its aggregate loan amount, the repayments stop. More financially successful members of the cohort support – in a clearly measurable way – less financially successful members.

In any case, we cannot see at all why the government should seek to make a profit on the interest on the loans, except for secondary purposes of selling off the loan book or making the costs to the taxpayer seem lower on the basis of arcane accounting devices. We have also been perplexed by the regressive nature of the current scheme, where middle-income graduates pay a higher total amount than the very well-off. If the government insists on setting interest rates well above its own costs of borrowing, it should in any case end the regressive nature of repayments. Recall that these arose since more successful individuals paid off the loans more rapidly, and thereby avoided the punitive interest rate. Students from better-off backgrounds might use parental contributions to avoid taking out the loans in the first place. Those who could afford it could even add their student loan to a commercially available fixed rate mortgage at a lower rate for a property purchase.

A way of avoiding these regressive effects is to assume that each graduate has taken out the full loan for the purposes of putting everyone on the same repayment scheme. The differential between any loan taken out and a full loan can be put into a notional account held by the government on behalf of the individual. Similarly, repayments by the individual are put into that account. The account should bear a real interest rate of zero. Then, at the specified terminal date of the loan (currently 30 years), the sum should be put to the loan and any residual returned to the individual. Under this procedure, the individual who has a high income and is repaying the loan early and thereby currently avoiding the punitive interest rates, or the individual with parental support who takes out a smaller loan or none at all, does not benefit relative to the lower income individual.

Student maintenance

The government has moved to a system where maintenance funding is handled in the same way as fees, with the student borrowing (up to) the full amount and repaying via the income-contingent loan. We have a number of problems with this in terms of equity and efficiency. For our expositional purposes, it does, however, have the simplifying feature that most of what we have said above about student loans can simply be carried forward to include maintenance, only doubling the figures involved. For a student living in accommodation in London, for example, the maintenance loans are roughly the same magnitude as current fees and treated in the same way in terms of repayment.

The amount of maintenance loan differs between London and the rest of the country, and upon whether or not the student is living at home or in accommodation. The amounts vary from about £7000 (living at home) to about £11,000 (living away from home in London). Our primary concern is for all students to make the right choice, given their preferences and qualifications, about where to go to university and about whether or not to live at home. We are not comfortable with students from lower-income families living at home either because of affordability or because of 'sticker shock' at the eventual loan amounts. We feel that it is particularly important that non-traditional students engage in the full university experience by living in student accommodation.

We would like to see support for widening participation in the form of ex ante grants for both maintenance and fees, not ex post writing-off of loans in 30 years' time. The importance of means-tested maintenance grants in encouraging participation has been demonstrated in a study by Dearden et al.[2] It is a daunting prospect for a family with a tradition of living hand to mouth to face a debt for fees even of £22,500 for a three-year course (under the fee reduction for all students that we favour). By returning to means-tested fee and maintenance support, available funds for subsidies are better targeted and also avoid rewarding failure. They are based upon limitations on the student's background support, financial and educational, and not upon any lack of effort or success on the part of the student – indeed, they reward the students from disadvantaged backgrounds who overcome these additional hurdles and achieve a place at university.

We have referred earlier to work done by London Economics for the Sutton Trust where they note various models for means testing. The particular model they use for illustration assumed current fee levels and a scheme where the wealthiest pay higher fees to subsidise the less advantaged. As a matter of principle, we do not think anyone should pay significantly above the costs of a public service and we favour lowering fees for all students. Any number of models are possible under assumptions of the end of the writing-off of loans and a zero real interest rate. Further, the £1000 per student currently claimed as spending on OFFA approved activities can be spent, we would argue more effectively, on means testing.

For example, assume for simplicity a fee level of £7500, and a maintenance loan of £7500 per year of study. Assume further that 10 per cent of students get a discount of 50 per cent and 10 per cent get a discount of 25 per cent. The total cost of the 50 per cent discount is then £750 per student across the whole cohort and the total cost of the 25 per cent discount is £375, making a total of £1125 per student across the whole cohort – a figure close to the money universities claim they are using for 'OFFA' supported activities. This means-tested support could therefore be supported just from re-directing those funds, and not even using our proposed savings from ending the non-repayment in the contingent-income loan system.

At these assumed levels for fees and maintenance for a three-year course a straightforward mortgage type scheme to pay back the loan over 40 years would cost the full-fee paying student £100 per month and £75 or £50 respectively for the discounted students. Any number of other models could be developed but this simple example shows the feasibility and – we would argue – clear desirability of this alternative to the current funding.

The upfront government funding in the 'mortgage scheme' could be arranged as at present through a loan company if the government wanted to continue the current accounting devices. Each graduate would have a personal account, repayments would be collected through the tax system with money accruing to the government current account and the graduate's account in the loan company credited. If the government, for accounting reasons, wished to sell off this student debt, it could still do so. In fact, this debt would be inflation index-linked, an asset class that is relatively absent from the market (except for existing government index-linked gilts), and for that reason would be attractive to pension and other investment funds.

When maintenance loans were increased to – for London students living in student accommodation – £11,000, it is perhaps not surprising that rents increased to roughly that amount! Student accommodation has become a lucrative business, with expansion in private and university provision. (This same phenomenon is apparent in the rocketing public cost of housing benefit following the transfer of large quantities of council housing stock to private landlords.) Some of the university provision has been monetised by selling off future revenue streams. Further, the inventory of student housing offered by a university will range from historical construction to new builds on newly acquired land, with very different costs to the institution. Students at UCL have gone on rent strikes and have achieved concessions from the university in terms of rent freezes on the lowest cost accommodation and significant bursaries to less well-off students.

Table 7.1: Weekly student accommodation and catering costs

Academic year	England	N Ireland	Scotland	Wales
2012	£176.40	£139.40	£183.26	£116.74
2013	£183.88	£136.10	£194.48	£124.50
2014	£196.10	£144.44	£200.51	£136.52
2015	£204.46	£147.73	£201.45	£137.84
2016	£211.46	£155.77	£194.14	£157.68

Source: HESA Estate Management Records 2012/13-2016/17

Due to data limitations (there is no direct data on rents), we construct Table 7.1 by taking rent and catering income and dividing by the number of bed spaces, and further allowing for a 40-week rental year. As can be seen, costs in England with a maximum maintenance loan of £6828 outside of London (for students from mid-income families) have risen sharply, compared in particular to Scotland where the loan is £4750. The figures in Table 7.1 will overstate the actual cost to a resident student since some catering income arises from non-resident students and staff. Nonetheless, this accurately shows the degree of inflation in these costs.

We favour some form of rent control, accepting the difficulties in implementation that are not unlike those currently facing housing associations or, historically, private rentals. However, if the government can regulate fees, it can also regulate the costs of accommodation. We would propose that each university be required to offer first year students single or double accommodation at centrally set rates (that differ across localities, as appropriate), with minimum standards set. We do not accept the current fear among economists about setting specific targets and rates. While there are potential inefficiencies, universities have a monopoly over on-campus housing, so there are also inefficiencies in uncontrolled rents. First year students, in our view, should prioritise living in on-campus housing, and are therefore particularly subject to monopoly pricing. What the regulatory agency should not do is micromanage and tell the university how to achieve the required availability and rent levels. If it is felt that a university needs to provide single accommodation in London to students for £150 a week, it is not for the regulatory agency to tell the university how best to do so, but simply to impose the rule upon the university.

Widening participation

Currently, universities agree a plan with OFFA and claim to be spending about £1000 per annum per student (out of fees paid by fellow students) on widening participation. We have argued that this money would be better spent on means-tested fees and maintenance grants. We feel that the activities of OFFA could be discontinued, with monitoring of achievements at improving access a direct responsibility of OfS – a task made easier by the data available from distribution of maintenance grants if these become means tested. This is consistent with our view that emphasis should be placed on results rather than micromanagement of process. Put more directly, since OFFA has not successfully generated widening participation in the system, and particularly at the more established universities, it has proved to be a waste of money. We note that the recent HEPI survey[1] shows wide gaps in the satisfaction rates of minority ethnic students compared to white students. Again, even on their own terms, the current arrangements are not 'fit for purpose'.

Achieving a greater diversity of background at top universities is not rocket science. Oxford University could fill its places with highly qualified state school students in proportion to the mixture in English schools as a whole, and not unduly rely upon those who have enjoyed a privileged private education. In saying this, we accept that admissions tutors at Oxford are admitting students fairly based upon traditional evaluations of 'merit', but we also accept the view of society that these measures and methods of determination may not be the best ones for a publicly-funded institution. In the same way, Oxford's students could reflect the social and ethnic make-up of England in general.

The question then becomes how best to achieve this diversity, not just for Oxford, but for other universities where the recruitment issue may be more difficult. We dismiss the essay writing and tick-boxes currently used in Access Agreements with OFFA as ineffective. This then leaves us with the standard methods for achieving a goal – taxes, subsidies or quantity targets – or coming up with a new proposal. We do not mind the imposition of taxes or subsidies, or even strict quantitative targets, but have decided on the following holistic proposal to address both the restoration of competition to the system and widening participation.

Our proposal is that the objectives of restoring competition and widening participation should be integrated in one simple mechanism. We begin with the first stage, which is to cap each university at its student numbers in 2011, when the higher fees came in, less 10 per cent. This will, given the growth in the system subsequently, have the greatest impact on the Russell Group, which has expanded disproportionately under the regime of uncapped numbers (and no effective OFFA intervention). We then allow each university to 'win back' its student numbers by admitting (and graduating) widening participation students, or – if it so desires and can compete effectively – go beyond its current numbers. We make no apology that – given their lower current numbers of widening participation students – the Russell Group would, if they don't compete, lose out the most. Widening participation students, under the means-tested regime we propose, will have been identified by their family household income. While it is possible to uncap only widening participation students, it is also possible to allow a university to enrol additional traditional-background students in proportion to the expansion in widening participation numbers.

All the government agency – the OfS – has to do to implement our proposals is to determine the actual base fee, the lower fee that can be set by primarily teaching institutions, a teaching grant to universities that choose to set a lower fee, and a teaching grant for specific subjects, the precise terms of fee and maintenance means testing, and any multiplier on additional overall numbers on top of widening participation numbers. We would suggest that the latter be greater than one, since some of the less advantaged students may be less well prepared than those who have benefited from 13 years of expensive private education. Universities must be prepared to give extra help if need be, particularly in the early stages of their university careers.

In Chapter Six, we gave the example of affordable housing in London and pitfalls that had to be avoided such as 'poor doors' where the individuals (often teachers and nurses) obtaining affordable flats were physically isolated from the purchasers of the more expensive properties. In the current system, students who repay their full loans end up subsidising the widening participation students. We feel that that is divisive. Under our proposal, the non-traditional students are not in the student number cap, so they are clearly additional and – because even a subsidised fee will likely be greater than marginal cost – are net contributors financially as well as academically and socially to the university. Further, if our proposal is followed and there is a multiplier applied – allowing additional traditional students for each non-traditional student – the direct benefit to all the students is enhanced. In these days of social media, the more non-traditional students recruited, the more places will become available for my Facebook friends from school, even if I'm from a traditional university attending background.

The risk or threat of bankruptcy

Universities rushed to spend the flood of extra funding in irreversible ways – they built new buildings. To those of us who care about architecture and design, this was a further unfortunate feature of the shift to the high fee environment. Rather than engaging in careful planning and rebuilding English universities with architectural innovation, there was a rush to build. Some of this was simply to keep up with others. It often looks as though some of the architects employed merged together disjointed schemes from different building plans already on their computers.

We do not suggest that UUK (the employers' body Universities UK) got together as a whole and decided to create a fait accompli that would require – with the increase in cost base – fees to remain at £9000 indefinitely with no caps on student numbers. However, economic equilibria – based upon the interactions of independent agents – often coordinate into what looks like a conspiracy!

This reality does, however, mean that, in considering policy changes, we have to confront the possibility that lowered funding will lead to bankruptcies in the system. We have looked at the increase in debt and in the ratio of debt to income (see Figures 7.1 and 7.2).

Figure 7.1: Debt in English universities

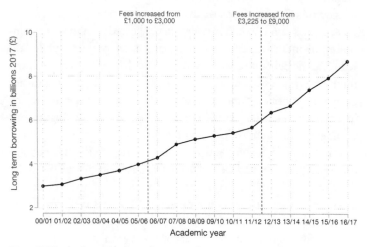

Note: HE institutions with fewer than ten students are excluded in this figure.

Source: HESA Finance Record 2000/01–2016/17

Figure 7.2: Debt relative to income

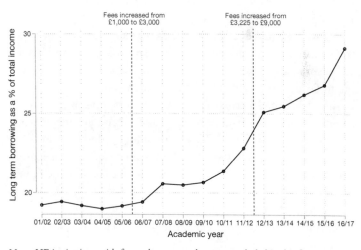

Note: HE institutions with fewer than ten students are excluded in this figure.

Source: HESA Finance Record 2001/02–2016/17

Although debt has gone up substantially, the overall ratio of debt to income remains at manageable levels of under 30 per cent. The increase in income would of course have allowed for a more prudent policy of increased debt for essential capital projects while still reducing the debt ratio. Some universities will have chosen to expose themselves more than others to the vagaries of student demand and government policy. Among large universities, the highest debt to income ratio in 2016/17 was about 100 per cent, with a significant number having debt to income of about 70 per cent.

The debt to income ratio may not be telling the full story of university exposure to risk. Thomas Hale wrote in the *Financial Times* on 7 February 2018 about the University of Swansea and its accommodation financing arrangements. University Partnerships Programme is a private provider that has arranged over £2 billion in new funding for university accommodation. It offers Special Purpose Vehicles for funding the accommodation, typically gaining the bulk of the student rents for a set time period (in the case of Swansea, 45 years), and structures the loan products into tiers with some of the loans guaranteed by the university (which is thereby taking on some of the risk). In effect, these arrangements are complicated mortgages that may not appear in the debt to income ratio we have described above.

Insofar as high debt and financial engineering exposure is due to the prudence or otherwise of particular institutions, and has not yet become a systemic problem, we note that no university is 'too big to fail' in the way that banks demanded and received bail-outs during the financial crisis. The OfS should be prepared – as were its predecessors – to arrange mergers and other adjustments when a particular institution had failed its students and staff by poor decision-making, and the OfS should move quickly to ensure good governmental practice at all institutions going into the future. Interestingly, the government White Paper in 2016[3] envisages the possibility of bankruptcy with a view to requiring institutions to have a plan for protecting students (but not staff or the institution) in case of exit.

Senior management salaries, academic salaries and pensions

There has been considerable negative press coverage over the high level of Vice Chancellor remuneration. The stakeholder model suggests that the dominant stakeholders will shift resources to follow their own preferences. Part of this may include their own remuneration. Although the governing body will have a Remuneration Committee, this often includes the Vice Chancellor. Even if the Vice Chancellor leaves the room when their own pay is discussed, they might feel inclined to support pay rises for the senior staff just below them (which not inconsequentially raises a base comparison for their own pay), and they will return to the room after the Committee determines their own pay (see Figures 7.3 and 7.4).

The data show significant pay rises for Vice Chancellors over the period, but even more dramatically for other senior managers. Interestingly, the pay of Vice Chancellors took off well before the fee rises. It may be that a preceding change in ethos to a more managerial approach led the sector to be receptive to the fee increases to £3000 and then £9000.

Figure 7.3: Vice Chancellor pay

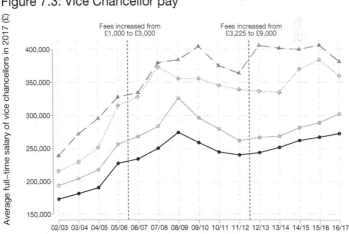

Source: Annual Vice Chancellor's Pay/Remuneration Survey, *Times Higher Education* 2004–18 (usually published in a Late spring edition).

Figure 7.4: Average senior management pay

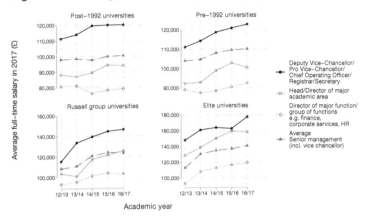

Source: HESA Staff Record 2012/13–2016/17

The American baseball player Babe Ruth is reported to have said, when confronted with the question why he was paid more than the President of the United States, 'I had a better year than he did.' The quality of management is vital to the success of an organisation – a university, a business or a football team is not a black box where inputs are entered and outputs naturally follow. Leadership matters. In fully competitive markets, Vice Chancellor and other senior management salaries might rise due to competition for the most outstanding and successful leaders. It is an empirical matter as to whether the increases in senior management pay are best explained as arising from vigorous competition for outstandingly successful individuals, or as a general push upwards in a managerial culture not directly related to improving the quality of education and research.

Although academic salary scales faced the public sector pay cap, there still remained the possibility for vigorous competition for the best researchers and teachers. Professorial scales are uncapped and a top, Nobel prize winning professor could – as in the US – make a salary in the hundreds of thousands of pounds. If teaching quality becomes the subject of fees-driven student demand, why shouldn't a notably good teacher similarly receive a very high salary? In fact, as we have observed, the sector has successfully contained the competition for academics and average real pay has significantly declined.

In terms of cost effectiveness, British universities are like the NHS in being relatively high quality for relatively low cost, and for much the same reason. Professional pay for the coalface workers – the doctors and the lecturers – is well below competitive market levels for individuals of high ability who have obtained high educational qualifications. Each system relies upon collegiality and the 'non-pecuniary' advantages of the post. For lecturers, the flexibility of the job and their ability to focus upon what they think is most important in their teaching and research is a large part of their pay-cheque. What a naïve Director of Human Resources might see as spare capacity to be exploited, or a troublesome lack of focus upon the NSS, is actually part of an efficient organisation of job tasks and time allocation. From a simple economic perspective, academic freedom is not just something to be valued on philosophical terms, but it is part of an overall compensation package.

Academics view their employment as being in the civil service model. Salaries are augmented by professional status and security. Effective academic freedom is only ensured by providing fairly ironclad employment security (once probation is passed). Otherwise a university could remove a lecturer espousing controversial or unpopular views under the guise of redundancy or through disciplinary and capability procedures. Although academic tenure was formally removed by Margaret Thatcher, it has remained effective at good universities both because it is fundamental to the mission and because it makes economic sense. A part of the differential in pay between an academic and a comparably educated and able individual in the private sector (such as in a financial firm in the City) is ascribable to this source.

Academics, like civil servants, also rely upon a secure and indeed generous pension scheme. Particularly given the public sector pay cap and the declining proportion of the university pay bill spent on academic salaries, along with the negative press coverage on Vice Chancellor pay packets, it seems a remarkable own goal for the sector to have (still unresolved) trade disputes over the pension system. Having already ended the final salary scheme in 2016, UUK sought to end defined benefits in total in 2018. Maintaining the scheme might involve an increase in employers' contributions of up to 7 per cent in the future, or – given the proportion of the relevant payroll in university budgets – an increase in overall budget costs of perhaps up to 2.5 per cent. This is clearly affordable, so resistance by Vice Chancellors must be more about the relationship between the different stakeholders in the university and the rise of 'managerialism'.

Returning the university to the academics and the students

When the government froze fees in October 2017, it became clear that overall university funding was likely to go down in real terms over the next few years, at least until demographics led to a rise in the number of 18 year olds. Further, the public sector pay cap is being relaxed, and academic salaries will therefore no longer decline at the same rate in real terms. Maintaining the pension scheme will require an increase in both employer and employee contributions. At the beginning of the book, we described the higher education sector as the lottery winner in public funding during a period of austerity. Reality is already beginning to seep into the discussions and universities are talking about cost cutting. Our own proposals are to jolt the system with real competition. Universities will have to earn back the revenue they now take for granted. They will need to offer a better product and ensure that their students are a diverse mix that reflects the make-up of England today.

Without a substantial shift in the funding system, universities are likely to respond with 'more of the same', mistaking 'marketing' for 'markets'. The academic payroll has gone down as a percentage of university expenditure and stands at about 30 per cent. These are the front-line staff. Trying to cut the academic side as real funding goes down would, in our view, be suicidal for the international standing and attractiveness to overseas students and businesses of our universities. In our view, universities can no longer afford large expenditure on marketing, whether it is spent on luxury student centres, expensive advertising or highly-paid senior administrators filling in TEF and Access submissions. This marketing is of zero sum benefit to the sector as a whole and of very little benefit to the students and the taxpayers who are being saddled with high levels of debt.

By focusing on the product – high quality education – we feel that universities can operate effectively in a system of 'just adequate resource'. In fact, it is a mystery why it was in the first place thought necessary to increase the teaching unit of resource by something of the order of 50 per cent on the basis of a professed aim to increase student numbers and improve the quality of education. Expansion with a constant unit of resource would in itself have produced a financial improvement since marginal expansion – if evenly spread across universities rather than concentrated in the Russell Group – can be achieved at marginal cost. This extra aggregate resource, rising with student numbers, could have been used for prudent refurbishment of the estate, improvements in SSRs and efforts to improve participation.

We have emphasised that the work of the university is done at the departmental level. The team is the academic staff, the technicians and the administrators within the department. Departmental administrators in particular tend to be on lower grades of the scale, and are the unsung heroes that largely determine the student experience. Students relate to the department, interact with the lecturers and other students, and often benefit from the administrators not only for their academic queries but for emotional and other support. All this happening at the departmental level avoids the anonymity and isolation that can lead students to feeling the levels of stress and inability to cope that have in turn led to serious student welfare concerns. One wonders why the increased demand for counselling is being met by more counselling staff rather than getting to the bottom of why there is such an increase in the first place.

At a time of just adequate resource a university must concentrate hard on its key priorities – teaching and research. Efficient professional administration is essential, but it is in service to the main objective. Concentration on the primary objective has the added bonus of improving the financial position through increasing research and consultancy income and attracting high quality overseas students, both undergraduate and post graduate. An administration cannot earn money, but an efficient, proportionate administration can ease the life of everyone in working to the common good. On the other hand, hiring one more administrator than strictly necessary is likely to create more work if new wheezes are proposed, more paperwork and meetings generated, more exchanges of correspondence and eventually demands for more administrative staff. All the administrative staffing for TEF and other government micromanagement has a multiplier effect, as administrators find the need to hire more administrators.

What appears to be unjustified growth in highly-paid, central administration can lead to resentment and an unfortunate divide in the community, undermining collegiality. But a deeper issue concerns management style. For example, a finance department has to be run on well-defined and documented procedures. Payroll has to work, cash flow managed, purchasing efficient, investments well managed. Each member of the administration has to know their clearly defined role and perform to procedures laid down by their line managers. Academic departments are different. Lectures and tutorials have to be given when promised, assignments marked with care and returned when promised. But how this is done is largely down to the individual, as is what goes into individual lectures and tutorials within the overall constraints of the agreed syllabus. This is not to say a department does not need managing, but a Head of Department's task and style differs from that of a first-rate head of administration, even though both should ensure humanity, commitment and collegiality within their departments. With the growth in university management, the previous essential role of academic heads in formulating policy has reduced. And the mode of management appropriate to the administration has increasingly been applied to the academic community.

Not only is this procrustean approach inappropriate and damaging to the overall liveliness of the community, it is also demotivating and inefficient. A well-motivated and proud academic department is more than willing to run school visits, field open days, engage with the media and so on, without coercion and without additional funding. Academics do not expect and do not get overtime pay. Satisfied students who identify with the care and concern of the academics and departmental staff are happy to go back to their schools to spread the word. But this requires a hands-off approach which is anathema to the controlled style of management perfectly appropriate for the administration. And the word soon gets out that this is a good place to be and so helps in the recruitment of new staff. It may give a Vice Chancellor sleepless nights wondering how things are going but they have appointed the academic staff and the least they can do is have confidence and let them get on with it.

It follows from this that paying the expanded administrative structure at high, commercial rates of pay is not only wasting public funds, but is demoralising for the institution as a whole. A Vice Chancellor's pay should be constructed relative to that of the university's leading professors, not to hypothetical managers in the banking and finance sector. There is no reason why any Vice Chancellor should be paid more than double the average rate of professors. Other senior academic officers should be fixed-term, part-time posts where the professor holding the assignment (such as Pro-Vice-Chancellor or Dean) goes back to their academic department, or decides to seek to become a Vice Chancellor elsewhere. It is this ability – after a period of additional service to their university – to return to their normal lives that encourages top researchers and teachers to take on administrative tasks and contribute to the strategic direction of the university.

In our view, students and the taxpayer can spend significantly less money and get not only better value, but a strictly better university education offering and academic environment.

Summary

We have taken the view that the current implementation of the market approach to universities, far from encouraging competition, leads to uniformity and top-down regulatory controls which are costly and counter-productive. For the final time in the book, we observe that we would not have gone down the market route at all. However, on its own terms – and we accept that the government of the day remains wedded to the market approach – the current system is inefficient and wasteful. For the purposes of our policy proposals, we have accepted not only the market system as envisaged by Browne, but even a constraint that no new taxpayer funds be added: we believe early years and schools are higher priorities.

Ironically, the 'market' has led to both less competition and more regulation. There has been a continued process of increasing government control over the last decades, from the UGC (University Grants Committee) being replaced by the UFC (Universities

Funding Council) and then HEFCE (Higher Education Funding Council for England) and now the OfS. Contradictions run throughout policy, with the government simultaneously arguing for greater 'academic freedom' and for the 'prevent strategy'. Our view is that universities work when they seek to achieve excellence and diversity, and are centres for vigorous debate and intellectual enquiry. The role of the government is to set up mechanisms and then get out of the way, without the sort of micromanagement and bureaucracy we have seen in the OFFA, NSS, TEF, and so on.

Effective economic mechanisms are simple but robust. We have the following main policy proposals:

1. Return competition to the system, and have real widening participation, by introducing caps on each university, but with uncapped numbers of students from non-traditional backgrounds, possibly with an overall student number multiplier to increase incentives to attract and support widening participation students.
2. Eliminate the rewards to failure in the current contingent-repayment loan scheme by having a mortgage type student funding scheme, but with means-tested fees and maintenance with a zero real rate of interest.
3. Give the Office for Students four main tasks. Restore the external examiner system as the method for ending grade inflation and guaranteeing the value of degrees. Ensure good and strong governance from the governing bodies. Continue to allocate special teaching grants for high cost subjects but extend this to subjects currently out of favour with students but important for the health of the system and the nation, such as, for example at present is the case with Modern Languages. Monitor participation rates and caps on student numbers.
4. Close down the OFFA and abandon the TEF and NSS.
5. Return base fees to a level more consistent with costs, of between £6000–£7500, to avoid wasteful expenditures.
6. Allow universities to set a reduced fee, with some of the differential made up from a block teaching grant.

Successive cohorts of students (often siblings) have been subject to changes in the cost of their education which will persist through their working lives. This is clearly unfair. How this is addressed and how the problem of paying off the existing long-term debt should be faced is a matter for government and beyond the scope of the task we have set ourselves. We feel strongly, however, that current policies have created complications, inefficiencies and unfairness and it is time for Occam's razor to be brought to the issue of university funding and fees.

Notes

1 Introduction

1 National Audit Office, 'The higher education market', 8 December 2017.

2 John Browne, 'Securing a sustainable future for higher education: an independent review of higher education funding and student finance', Department for Business, Innovation and Skills, 12 October 2010.

3 Nicholas Stern, 'Building on success and learning from experience: an independent review of the research excellence framework', Department for Business, Energy and Industrial Strategy, July 2016.

4 Bahram Bekhradnia and Diana Beech, 'Demand for higher education to 2030', *HEPI Report* 105, 15 March 2018.

2 How Did We Get Here?

1 The Robbins Report, *Higher education*, HMSO, 1963.

2 The Dearing Report, *Higher education in the learning society*, HMSO, 1997.

3 Full discussions of the history of the debate over student fees are given in Nicholas Hillman, 'From grants for all to loans for all: Undergraduate finance from the implementation of the Anderson Report (1962) to the implementation of the Browne Report (2012)', *Contemporary British History*, 27, 3, 249–70; and in Robert Anderson, 'University fees in historical perspective', *History and Policy*, February 2016, www.historyandpolicy.org/policy-papers/papers/university-fees-in-historical-perspective.

4 Public Accounts Committee 41st report of 2014/2015 session, 'Financial support for students at alternative higher education providers', 24 February 2015.

3 Markets Without Competition

1 Andrew Jenkins and Alison Wolf, 'What's in a name? The impact of reputation and rankings on the teaching income of English universities', *Higher Education Quarterly*, 2018, 1–18.

4 Stakeholders and Expenditures

[1] Nicholas Stern, 'Building on success and learning from experience: An independent review of the research excellence framework', Department for Business, Energy and Industrial Strategy, July 2016.

5 Expanding Numbers and Maintaining Standards

[1] Office for National Statistics, User Requested Data: Percentage of employed graduates in non-graduate roles, parts of the UK, 2015 to 2017, 26 April 2018, reference number 8381.

[2] Quality Assurance Agency, *UK Quality Code for Higher Education, Part A*, October 2014, p26.

[3] Claire Crawford and Wenchao Jin, *Payback time? Student debt and loan repayments: What will the 2012 reforms mean for graduates*, Institute of Fiscal Studies, April 2014.

[4] Office for Budget Responsibility, Fiscal sustainability analytical paper: Student loans update July 2016 and each preceding July since 2011.

[5] Paul Johnson (IFS), 'The murky world of student loans, the national debt and a fiscal illusion', *The Times*, 19 February 2018.

6 Widening Participation and Student Finance

[1] Carl Cullinane and Rebecca Montacute, 'Fairer fees: Reforming student finance to increase fairness and widen access', *The Sutton Trust*. November 2017.

[2] Ron Johnston, 'England's new scheme for funding higher education through student fees: "Fair and progressive"?', *The Political Quarterly*, 84, 2, July 2013, 200–10.

[3] Paul Johnson (IFS), 'The murky world of student loans, the national debt and a fiscal illusion', *The Times*, 19 February 2018.

[4] Ron Johnston, David Manley, Kelvyn Jones, Anthony Hoare and Richard Harris, 'British educational trajectories from school to university: Evaluating quantitative evidence in policy formulation and justification', *Policy and Politics*, 45, 2, April 2017, 137–55.

[5] Ron Johnston, David Manley, Kelvyn Jones, Anthony Hoare and Richard Harris, 'University admissions and the prediction of degree performance: an analysis in the light of changes to the English schools' examination system', *Higher Education Quarterly*, 70, 1, 2016, 24–42.

[6] Iris Bohnet, *What Works: Gender Equality by Design*, Cambridge: Belknap Press, March 2016.

[7] David Dickinson, 'The carrot vs the stick in work team motivation', *Experimental Economics*, 4, 1, June 2001, 107–24.

[8] Richard S. Ruch, *Higher Ed, Inc.: The Rise of the For-profit University*, Baltimore, MD: Johns Hopkins University Press, 2003.

7 Adjusting to the Future

[1] Jonathan Neves and Nick Hillman, *2018 Student academic experience survey*, Advance HE and HEPI.

[2] Lorraine Dearden, Emla Fitzsimons and Gill Wyness, 'The impact of tuition fees and support on university participation in the UK', *Institute for Fiscal Studies Working Paper* W11/17, September 2011.

[3] Gov.UK, *Success as a knowledge economy: teaching excellence, social mobility and student choice*, 16 May 2016 (www.gov.uk/government/publications/ higher-education-success-as-a-knowledge-economy-white-paper).

Index

Note: page numbers in *italic* type refer to Figures; those in **bold** type refer to Tables.